" "

What they're saying about the book:

"An easy to read book loaded with numerous, practical ideas for turning cold calls into prospects and customers. A must read for anyone who needs to prospect to make sales!" – **Dr. Tony Alessandra**, author of *Non-Manipulative Selling* and *The Platinum Rule*

"With *Cold Calling for Cowards*, Jerry Hocutt has done something remarkable. He's turned an activity that most find difficult into one that is rewarding." – **Robert Cialdini**, author of *Influence: Science and Practice* and Regents' Professor of Psychology and Marketing, Arizona State University

"This book will put steel in your spine, ice water in your veins, and gravel in your guts. It will make you unstoppable!" – **Brian Tracy**, author of *The Psychology of Selling*

"If the thought of a cold call makes you break into a sweat, *Cold Calling for Cowards* is for you. Jerry landed his job with McCaw Communications by telling the sales manager that 'Cold calling sucks!' He then went on to lead the nation in sales for three years. Who better to learn from??? In this easy to read, practical book, Jerry shares *The Secret* he learned to become #1 in sales so that you can do the same." – **Susan RoAne**, professional speaker and author of *How To Work A Room*® and *What Do I Say Next?*

"Highly recommended. Jerry Hocutt has a proven track record in sales and is the authority on the subject of cold calling. This is a book of substance – not hype. Everything Jerry talks about has been used successfully by thousands of his Cold Calling for Cowards® students." – **Roger Dawson**, author of *Secrets of Power Negotiating*

"In this book, Jerry Hocutt presents many concepts that sales profession-als and selling teams can use to help them succeed. In addition to en-couraging a positive mindset and effective skill set development, he em-phasizes the importance of organizing and managing the many contact and sales opportunity details that are required for developing valuable prospects and strong customer relationships." – **Joe Bergera**, ACT! by Sage, Senior Vice President and General Manager, Sage Software

"*Cold Calling for Cowards* transforms the faint-hearted into the undaunt-ingly courageous cold caller. In this thoroughly enjoyable and insightful book, Jerry Hocutt eliminates the fear factor and offers a treasure-trove of do-able ways to *connect* with customers. So many good tips for any-one at any level of sales experience. After reading this book you'll want to run to the phone and start calling!" – **Rebecca Z. Shafir**, author of *The Zen of Listening*

"I have made a lot of cold calls. They are not fun. If you have to grow your sales, you have to get it done. This book will give you the right atti-tude and the right tools to make it happen." – **Richard Lowe**, President, Sir Speedy, Inc.

"It's interesting to see how you voice everyone's concerns about cold calling and how you help us realize that we are not the only ones who find it difficult. Your book is a road map to get us where we want to go. You make the reader aware of the pitfalls and how to constantly change them to make each call more productive and to make us feel better about what we are doing. That is the first step to success." – **Rosalie A. Bu-lach**, Founder & CEO, Name-Finders Lists, Inc.

"Practically everyone hates to be rejected. It's human nature. That is probably why cold calling is so difficult for so many people. Jerry Hocutt teaches you how to make those cold calls enthusiastically without the fear of being rejected by anyone at the other end of the phone. He teaches you how to make that initial communication which can be in-valuable in both your business and in your personal life." – **Dr. Lillian Glass**, author of *Talk to Win; Toxic People – 10 Ways of Dealing With People Who Make Your Life Miserable;* and *I Know What You're Think-ing – Using the 4 Codes of Reading People To Improve Your Life*

"Who ever thought cold calling could be fun? Only Jerry Hocutt. But read his book and you'll become a believer. Plus two other things. You'll laugh a lot (that's one) and you'll get more appointments out of the cold calls you make (that's two)." – **Kevin Daley**, author of *Socratic Selling: How to Ask Questions That Get the Sale*

What they're saying about the seminars:

"Hocutt's paying audience knows the truth: Calling strangers for a living can be hell. They are the foot soldiers in America's business-to-business selling game. And Hocutt is their drill sergeant. His plain-spokenness wins people over." – *Los Angeles Times*, "He's the Zen Master of Cold Calls"

"Hocutt certainly can ease the pain from perhaps one of the most dreaded duties in the business world: the cold call." – *The Star-Ledger*, New Brunswick, NJ, "The Lord of the Rings"

Cold Calling for Cowards

Cold Calling for Cowards

Jerry Hocutt

Chugwater Publishing

For more information on sales and marketing, visit our website www.Cold CallingForCowards.com.

To receive our free weekly sales and marketing newsletter, sign-up at www.ColdCallingForCowards.com.

First printing 2007

Hocutt, Jerry
    Cold calling for cowards: how to turn the fear of rejection into opportunities, sales, and money. – 1st edition.
Includes bibliographical references and index.

ISBN 978-0-615-13875-6
Library of Congress Control Number 2007900217
    I. Sales – United States. Hocutt, Jerry. II. Title

Cold Calling for Cowards is a registered trademark of Hocutt & Associates, Inc.

Edited by Michael L. Hocutt

Cover Design by Christopher Gaal, Crazybridge Studios

*Dedicated to everyone who gathers the courage
to create their own opportunities
and make a difference*

ACKNOWLEDGEMENTS

People attending our Cold Calling for Cowards® seminars know that ours is a family business. Without my family's dedication, loyalty, and belief in our purpose to help people in business improve their lives, business, and sales, the seminars and this book would have never happened. As the speaker I've been fortunate to get the attention – but it's the family behind the scenes that did the real work to make it happen.

My wife, Linda, has held the family and business together through her tireless and patient efforts to keep everyone calm and focused. She's the reason I got into the business. "If you think you can do better, do your own seminars," she scolded me after I whined about poor training from another's program. No sympathy; but she pointed me to a new opportunity.

Daphne Slife is our oldest daughter and was our first employee. She dared to venture into the two unknowns: starting a business with nothing but an idea, and working with her dad. Gutsy. Her husband Eric became our marketer, seminar planner, and negotiator. Our other daughter Jana Lacroix brought us her work ethic, creative marketing skills, and her enjoyment of driving for the thousands of miles between seminar cities. (I think my cutting that funeral procession off on the Interstate had something to do with her desire to get behind the wheel.) Jana's husband, Fletcher, later joined our group and has undertaken every job assigned to him from traveling, to seminar planning, to computer guru.

My sister Jo Anne Hocutt has been nothing but a pleasure to work with even though she made us cringe when she kept yelling "Wooo! Wooo! Wooo!" when we took her to her first Broadway play. Peggy Slife took registrations, traveled, and flew out in the middle of the night to help us in emergencies; she's always the gracious hostess. I'm grateful to my niece Diana Hocutt and to my brother Mike and sister-in-law Sarah Hocutt for all their seminar trips, support, and creative ideas. Thanks to Eldon Slife for his volunteerism, for free room and board while we were on the road, and for his sense of direction in picking us up at the KC airport.

To my grandchildren who were too young to participate in the seminars, they gave us all a reason to look forward to making those long trips home in the middle of the night after being on the road: Jacob and Savannah Slife, and Bailey and Lily Lacroix. To my granddog Banjo: Fetch!

Thanks, too, to the hundreds of salespeople, managers, service people, business owners, customers, and – yes – even competitors I've been lucky to work with who have taught me as much about myself as they taught me about selling. Your ideas, insights, and humor continue to inspire me even though you may never know it.

Most importantly, I especially want to thank the thousands of people across America who have attended our seminars and who have given me the opportunity to meet you, learn from you, and share your experiences with our thousands of readers and students. As I teach what little I know, I can attest to a message I saw on a school's reader board: "Teaching is learning twice."

Go. Teach. Learn.

Like a compass,

      I can point you in the right direction.

            But I can't take you there.

What's in It for You?

"I could sell to anyone – if I could just get in front of them first." This book gets you in front of them.

George, a trader at Bank of America where I was doing sales training, told me after one of our sessions, "Jerry you teach like Harvey Penick."

"I hope that's a compliment," I said, "because I don't know who Harvey Penick is."

"Evidently, you don't play golf," George replied. "He's from your hometown of Austin, Texas. Anyone who's ever been anyone in golf – male or female – has traveled from around the world to take lessons from Harvey. He used to be the golf coach at the University of Texas. He was the golf pro at the Austin Country Club. When Ben Crenshaw knelt to pray on the 18th green after winning his second Masters, he was praying for Harvey Penick who passed away the week before.

"I'll send you one of Harvey's books, *And If You Play Golf, You're My Friend: Further Reflections of a Grown Caddie*, and tell me if you don't agree that you teach like Harvey."

Two weeks later the book arrived with a note inside. "Thank you for your insights," he wrote, "my business has picked up substantially. Best month ever. Enjoy the book. George."

Inside the book, George marked the passages where he compared me to Harvey Penick. I'm humbled that George would put me in the same league as Mr. Penick.

When people went to Harvey for their first lessons, he would tell them the same thing. "I'm not going to make you rich. And I'm not going to make you famous. I don't teach theory. *I teach simple things that produce good results*."

George got it. The purpose of this book, of my seminars, is not to make you rich. Or famous. I don't teach theory. I teach simple, proven things like the 3800/6 technique, or the Coward technique, or the Fonz technique that produce good results.

And like Harvey Penick's protégés, it's up to you to take your swings.

Contents

Cold Calling Sucks!

1. **Two Silly Questions**
    Then One Question to Test Your Honesty 1

2. **Scaring Your Pants Off**
    You Know What I'm Talking About ....…........... 3

3. **Call Reluctance**
    It's Not Important Why We Have It ...…............. 7

4. **Batter Up!**
    Give Yourself the Opportunity 14

5. **Hey-y-y-y!**
    Cool ....…… 16

6. **Coward**
    Semper Fi ....…... 20

7. **Edgar Martinez**
    My, oh My! 25

8. **I Don't Have the Time to Cold Call**
    Oops! Now You Do. 28

9. **Paradox of Cold Calling**
    Don't Try to Find Customers 31

10. **The Doctor Is In**
    Rx for Listening 33

11. **The #1 Complaint of Customers**
   Why Men Can't Watch The View 37

12. **Would You Like Me to Wash That Brain
   for You?**
   Will You Need Bleach? 40

13. **How to Think on Your Feet Faster**
   You Couldn't Buy a Better List of Prospects 48

14. **Listen Up!**
   Gatekeepers Are Giving Clues 57

15. **In the Blink of an Eye**
   Snorkeling with Socrates 59

16. **Did I Say That?**
   Don't Commit Vocal Suicide 64

17. **Monster Truck Extravaganza Voice**
   Go for It! 67

18. **Not Fair But True**
   Don't Let Your Voice Give You Away ....…. 69

19. **One Ring-y Ding-y**
   The Dork Factor 72

20. **Shooting from the Lip**
   You've Got 20 Seconds 75

21. **End Run Around Gatekeepers**
   8 Options to Score 82

22. **The Eliminator**
   Voicemail: Love It or Leave It? 93

23. **Voicemail Jail Break**
   How to Create Your Voicemail Script 103

24. **Getting Rid of the Blahs**
   *If You're Going to Send a Letter
   Before You Call* 106

25. **The Best Question to Ask on a First Sales Call**
   Revealing Personalities 111

26. **It Seemed Simple at the Time**
   The One Who Makes the Fewest Mistakes Wins ... 116

27. **Only the Persuaded Can Persuade**
   What Are You Thinking? 122

28. **Famous Quotes**
   Did the Three Stooges Ever Reject a Script? 129

29. **Your Honor, I Object!**
   Oh? 137

30. **How to Be #2 Until You're #1**
   *Get Your Foot in the Door without Getting
   It Crushed* 144

31. **I'll Cut You Off at the Knees**
   Psychics, Psychos, and Columbo 149

32. **I'll Get Back to You**
   And Other Fairy Tales 159

33. **30 Seconds to Crash and Burn**
   Lights! Camera! Action! 171

34. Good to See You Again…eh…Bill? Bob? John? Shirley?
Nuts! How to Remember Names Better …………... 178

35. Mirror, Mirror on the Wall
Hell's Angels ……………………………………….. 186

36. Queen to Knight's f3
Are You Crazy? ………………………….……… 190

37. It's Not Magic
If You Know How It's Done ………………………... 193

38. Six Hours?
Man, I Could Have Done This in 20 Minutes! …... 197

39. Sleight of Hand
The Most Important Contact ……………………….. 207

40. Palm Down
Put-Down Artist …………………………………… 213

41. Palm Up
Put Them at Ease, Get Their Trust ……………… 218

42. The Dreaded Dead Fish
That Stinks! …………………………………………… 220

43. Politician
Show Me the Money! ……………………………….. 223

44. The Traveling Arm
Don't Touch Me! Don't! Don't Do It! …………..... 226

45. The Half-Hand
Back Off! ……………………………………………… 228

46. Bone-Crusher
  Secret from the Florida Highway Patrol 232

47. To Shake or Not to Shake
  The Rest of the Story 234

48. Which Part of the Anatomy Was That?
  Things They Never Taught You in Biology 241

49. In Search of the Holy Grail
  Treasure It. Guard It. But Use It. 249

Appendix A
  A Program to Increase Your Referrals
  *Referral Secrets from the #1 Salesman in the
  World* 251

Appendix B
  Positioning Yourself to Be #2
  *How to Make the Short List Without Becoming a
  Pest* 255

Appendix C
  Increasing Customer Retention
  It's About Staying Connected 257

Appendix D
  Do Not Call Registry
  Didn't the Federal Government Ban Cold Calling? .. 260

Index 261

Bibliography 265

Okay. Who's Responsible for This? 268

Interview the Author
  Invite Me to Your Sales Meeting. Media Requests? ... 269

Cold Calling Sucks

There. Feel better?

I agree. (Don't show this to your sales manager.)

Those three words landed me my job at the Fortune 1000 McCaw Communications' Telepage Northwest. (Craig McCaw has since sold his company to AT&T for a few billion.) Within minutes on the first interview Paul, the sales manager, asked me, "What do you think about cold calling?"

That wasn't a deep question. The answer jumped off my tongue before my brain could slam on the brakes.

"Cold calling sucks."

I waited until he wiped the surprised look off his face and then added, "But I'm one of the best you'll ever see do it."

When the *Los Angeles Times* called me the *Zen Master of Cold Calls*, I thought, "Man, I'm screwed. Now everyone will think that I enjoy doing it."

I still don't. But I do it because it works.

I set company records by becoming the #1 salesman in the nation and salesman of the year for three years. I made more sales from cold calling AND referrals every year than any other salesperson. Does cold calling work? Yes. Do you have to love doing it? No.

But there is one truth about cold calling: people don't want to know how to cold call better. They don't want to cold call – period. However, until you come up with a better plan that gets you customers quickly, or get out of sales altogether, it won't hurt to add it to your repertoire.

Knock, knock. Who's there?
What attracts my attention shall have it, as I will go to the man who knocks at my door, while a thousand persons as worthy go by it, to whom I give no regard.
- Ralph Waldo Emerson

This is a book of hundreds of techniques I've learned from professionals through over 30 years of selling. They work for me, and I know they work for the thousands who have attended our seminars. They're small things that produce results.

Someone in your territory is buying what you're selling today. Your job is to find them before they find your competitors.

1

Two Silly Questions

Then One Question to Test Your Honesty

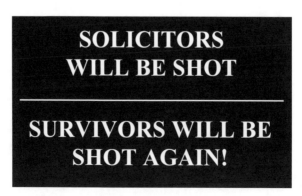 **Q**uestions like these are important when you're cold calling, but I won't tell you why until later in the book.

First silly question: Do you like to have fun? Tap this page once if you do. Go ahead. No one's looking.

Done? Good.

Second silly question: Are you open to new ideas? Tap this page twice if you are. Go ahead. Don't make me have to come after you.

SOLICITORS
WILL BE SHOT

SURVIVORS WILL BE
SHOT AGAIN!

Good job.

Now one question to test your honesty. Tell me the truth even if your sales manager is peering over your shoulder. If given the choice, wouldn't you really rather *not* have to cold call to find new customers? Be truthful. Tap this page three times if you agree.

That's enough. Stop tapping. Stop it!

Remember these questions. We'll come back to them later.

2

Scaring Your Pants Off

You Know What I'm Talking About

Merriam-Webster defines a *cold call* as "a telephone call soliciting business made directly to a potential customer without prior contact or without a lead."

That's so 60's.

Even if you throw in that a cold call includes a "*walk-in call* to a company to solicit business", the definition still doesn't carry water today.

My **definition of cold calling**: initiating any type of contact that scares you or makes you feel uncomfortable in order to sell yourself, your service, or your product and puts you in a position to be rejected. Cold calling is manifested by salespeople performing avoidance tasks, catching up on their paperwork, or plain ole' BS'ing.

One of our new sales trainees returned to the office after his first morning to solo in the field doing walk-in cold calls. He started clearing out his desk. I asked him what was going on.

"I pulled up to the office complex," he stated, "parked the car, set the brake – and sat there in my car for two hours. TWO HOURS! I couldn't move. I was shaking. I was sweating. I was hyperventilating. I couldn't move."

"For two hours?" I asked incredulously.

"Couldn't move. Man, I can't sell if this is what it takes to find new business. It's just not for me. I'm quitting."

That's a cold call. You know what I'm talking about.

Well…the 60's version of a cold call anyway. Today's cold calling goes way beyond scaring your pants off. Today, the cold call is used to start the relationship. Once you start the relationship, you better have a plan to grow and nurture it. Cold calls don't sell. Relationships sell.

The cold call is like diving off the high board into a spring-fed pool like Barton Springs in Austin, Texas. Once you get over the initial shock, then you swim.

Cold calling aliases

Telephone and walk-in calls to strangers definitely qualify as cold calls. But there are other business contacts camouflaged under a variety of names that cause as much discomfort.

Remember that last seminar you attended? What did you do once you signed in and picked up your workbook? Got your coffee, politely nodded to the stranger in line with you, and then found your seat.

Before the program began, you may have buried your head in your newspaper or workbook to avoid making eye contact with others. Maybe you got on your cell phone to make that call that just couldn't wait.

If you saw other attendees "working the room" you were silently praying, "Don't come near me. Don't talk to me. Keep away." If you were with a friend or group, you didn't venture far to introduce yourself to your neighbors in the front or back of you.

Don't feel bad. You're not alone. 90% of people are afraid to introduce themselves to strangers. Networking is cold calling in disguise.

Awww...shucks
93% of adults think of themselves as being shy.
> *- Susan RoAne*

Cocked and loaded

Salespeople working trade show booths are cold calling. Their companies pay huge sums of money to get them to connect with show attendees. But they don't. Meeting strangers makes them uncomfortable.

92% of booth masters are shooting themselves in the foot and they never feel the pain. (That's right. Your salespeople are cocked and loaded. Break out the flak jackets.) They hide behind their booths and don't take the initiative to walk over and introduce themselves to strangers. Yet 76% of people who meet the salesperson will remember his or her name and be more open and talkative.

Worse still, of those people who toss their business cards into the fishbowl on the counter, most have something the salesperson wants: a problem in search of a solution. And the card often belongs to the decision-maker who has money in the budget. Yet 86% are never contacted; their phone never rings.

Your cross-selling sucks

Even contacting our own customers to sell more of what we have makes us uncomfortable. Why don't more salespeople cross-sell?

Mark Stevens, *Your Marketing Sucks*, says it's because we feel it's "not professional", it makes us "uncomfortable doing it", and we feel it's "too pushy". We have a chance to grow our business, but don't because we're uncomfortable. Cross-selling is a *nom de plume* for cold calling.

Cold calling for referrals

Sales managers can't understand why their salespeople don't ask for referrals. Referrals are the best way to increase their sales.

But asking for referrals is nothing more than cold calling for leads; it makes us uncomfortable. Even when referrals are given, 50% are never called. Why? Salespeople have to initiate contact with a stranger – cold call.

Cold calling is no longer about getting a list of unknown names, calling them, and speed talking. Cold calling today is about initiating contact, building relationships, and keeping in touch.

We hate to cold call. We don't make the effort to build relationships. And we hope for the best.

Good luck with that.

3

Call Reluctance

It's Not Important *Why* We Have It. We Have It.
It's Important How We *Handle* It.

 Three factors contribute to our call reluctance.

1. We don't believe we can find customers by cold calling.
2. Our fear of rejection.
3. We don't have the courage to act.

This chapter looks at the first factor: we don't believe we can find customers.

One of our seminar attendees in Pennsylvania sent me a newspaper article written by a well-known author I respect. My friend wanted to know what I thought about the author's comments.

The author had some good points. He didn't like cold calling and he was listing his reasons why it doesn't work.

First, he said, they don't know you. True, but isn't that the purpose of cold calling? To introduce yourself so they'll get to know you. That's why we network. Advertise. Work trade shows. To get known. And what faster and more inexpensive way is there than cold calling?

The author said, "They probably already have what you are selling." Hey, this is great. This is what I call a Level 2 prospect we'll discuss later. Bad advice if you're in real estate, printing, or communications sales. Besides, what are the chances of finding someone who doesn't already own what you sell? What? They'll never buy again? Are they forever locked in to one vendor?

Ain't That the Truth?
People who think they know everything are
very irritating to those of us who do.
- Unknown

"It's the worst-trained skill by companies," the author goes on. Can't disagree. You can't train what you don't know. That's certainly helped our Cold Calling for Cowards® seminar business.

"It creates an atmosphere of repeated rejection." True again. It's like speed dating. It's designed for rejection. But that's what separates professional salespeople from order takers. We know there's going to be rejection. It's part of the game. Do you think a boxer would ever step into the ring assuming he'd never get hit hard and often? He expects it and he trains for it.

"It's the single biggest cause of salespeople quitting." True again. But it's the glass half-full. It keeps people out of the sales profession and cuts down on your competition.

At one of my previous jobs I took a recent college grad, who was interviewing for a sales position with our company, on some walk-in cold calls with me. Pulling back into the parking lot after three hours in the field, she leaned over and said to me, "Tell your sales manager I'm not coming back in for the rest of the interview. If this is what you have to do to sell, I have no interest in being in sales." From that day forward, we always included taking sales candidates out into the field with us for cold calls before the second interview. We eliminated a lot of wannabe's and saved our resources to spend elsewhere.

The author went on. "No preparation, just go 'dial for dollars' or 'pound on doors.'" Again, he's right. But this proves my point to sales managers who believe that cold calling is a numbers game. It's not. It's a numbers *and skills* game.

For example, I can't play baseball. If I'm standing in the batter's box facing Cy Young Award winner Randy Johnson, there's no way I can make a living playing professional ball. He's too good, and I'm too bad. I don't care how many swings (numbers) I take at the ball, I'll never get a hit. However, if I were younger, dedicated, and acquired and used the necessary skills, maybe I could make a living in the big leagues.

The same is true for cold calling. You have to acquire the skills and use those skills if you want to be successful.

I See the Light
There are no rules here—we're trying to accomplish something.
- Thomas Edison

Finally, the author asked, "Would you rather have 100 people to cold call or two referrals?" And the article ends. That's a silly question. Who wouldn't want two referrals? But to be fair to the author, he's like many others who write in the same vein. They all say referrals are the best way to get business, but then they *never tell you how to get them*. I show you how. See ***Appendix A*** ("A Program to Increase Your Referrals – Referral Secrets from the #1 Salesman in the World" for a referral program that's proven to work for you.)

What the author fails to point out is that we're cold calling all our lives. I met my wife 40 years ago because I cold called her to get a date. I had to cold call a real estate agent to get him to sell us a house. Had to cold call a car salesman to buy our car. Cold call an attorney to get him to help us set up our business. Remember, cold calling is initiating any type of contact that scares you or makes you uncomfortable. That's why many people are reluctant to change vendors. They have to cold call to try and give their money away and it scares them to talk with new people.

So if we're cold calling to buy something, why not take it up a notch and cold call to find someone who needs our help to help them solve their problems? The good news: your competitors are not. By hiding behind the phone, they're conceding more business to you. This is your opportunity. Seize it.

Three reasons cold calling doesn't work

1. We don't want to cold call.
2. We don't have the right attitude about cold calling.
3. We don't have the skills for cold calling.

If you don't want to cold call, I can't help. Please stop reading now and give this book to someone who wants to take the initiative to help others. I won't try to convert you or do missionary work with you. If your mind is made up, there's nothing I can say that will change it. Some future events may make you change your mind.

But if you don't have the right attitude about cold calling, this book can help. Instead of thinking of cold calling as being drudgery or something to be afraid of, think of cold calling as being like your favorite mystery book. And who doesn't love a good mystery? They're full of suspense. Surprises. Unpredictable outcomes. They're scary. They're full of clues to be solved. They get the adrenalin flowing. Just like cold calling.

Finally, for the skills you need for cold calling, this book can definitely help. Cold calling, like the professional batter, is about doing the right things, at the right time – and getting better at it.

Lessons from the Food Network

But before we explore the required skills of cold calling, let's look at one other thought that may be lurking in the recesses of your mind. I know it bothered me at one time. Running out of prospects. We're afraid that if we run out of prospects to call on, we'll run out of customers. Run out of customers and we have to quit our job and start all over again.

When I started selling at McCaw Communications that thought occurred to me. Each sales territory had only two to three zip codes. And we had to share that territory with another salesperson; we were competing with each other. That meant both of us had to sell enough product to not only meet our quotas, but to make the amount of money that would make us happy. Was it possible? Or would I be looking for another job all too soon?

That's when I discovered my *Recipe for Finding Customers*. I was already familiar with the *Cake Theory of Finding Customers* that our salespeople subscribed to. The Cake Theory goes something like this: there's only one cake (our prospect base) and it's only so big. Once each slice of the cake is taken away (a salesperson converts a prospect into a customer), the cake disappears. Jobs to follow. In order to preserve the cake we'd make fewer cold calls, thus saving the cake and our jobs.

BAM!
It's not rocket science.
- Emeril Lagasse

Slowly the dawn came. Why not be the chef with the recipe? Then I could make all the cakes I wanted. I did. You have the recipe, too. Here it is.

1. Look on the Internet or in the Yellow Pages and count the number of competitors you have in your territory.
2. Take an educated guess as to how many salespeople each competitor has in your territory. Assume they have as many salespeople as your company.
3. Determine their quotas. Assume they're the same as yours.
4. Do the math. How many of your services or products are being sold in your territory each month? In my territory alone at McCaw, 1500 of our products were being sold each month. My quota was only 40. That meant that 1460 of my products were being sold by my competitors every month in my territory. Understanding this, I couldn't cold call and get rejected fast enough. I had to find the prospects before they found and called my competitors. I would never

run out of prospects. BUT WAIT! THERE'S MORE! (Got to love those infomercials.)

5. There's an attrition of customers (yours and your competitors') every month. This adds to your prospect base.

6. Your competitors (companies and salespeople) come and go. When that happens, they leave behind orphaned customers in search of new sources. Your prospect base expands.

7. New services, products, and prices are introduced every month, creating new needs, new prospects, and new markets. You have an endless supply of prospects.

STOP THE MADNESS! I CAN'T STAND IT! SO MANY PEOPLE TO CALL, SO LITTLE TIME!

Never again fear someone coming into your territory and "stealing" one of your prospects. You have the recipe. Go out and make some more.

Now, what are we going to do about our fear of rejection? Turn the page.

4

Batter Up!

Give Yourself the Opportunity

The second cause of call reluctance is the fear of rejection.

Without getting into the details of Neuro-Linguistic (brain-language) Programming here's a quick way to use the technique to deal with your fear of rejection when cold calling.

In a layman's nutshell, psychologists John Grinder and Richard Bandler, creators of NLP, said that if you're not happy with the results that you're getting, simply change the pictures that you're making to yourself.

When you change your pictures, you change your feelings, which change your attitude, which change your actions, which change your results.

For example, when you're cold calling and you're staring at that 300 pound telephone what pictures come to mind? Do you see yourself defeated? Embarrassed? Head down, shoulders slumped? Do you feel rejected before you even start?

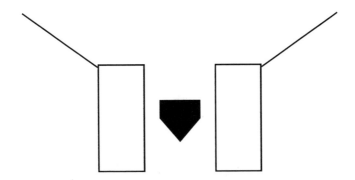

Try this. I keep a picture of a batter's box on a 3x5 card taped above the telephone. It reminds me that making cold calls is like playing baseball. When I look at that card it reminds me of Babe Ruth. Ruth had a lifetime batting average of .342. That meant that every time he stepped into the batter's box, he had a 66% probability of getting put out. But that was okay. The connecting 34% made him a legend.

The Bambino knew he had to step into that batter's box by himself. He had to take the swings by himself. He had to acquire the skills necessary to get the job done. He had to improve with each swing of the bat.

The same with cold calling. You'll fail more than you'll succeed. You'll have to do it by yourself. You'll have to acquire the skills to be successful. But you'll get better with each call. And like Ruth, you're giving yourself the opportunity to succeed.

When you look at the telephone, don't see it as an instrument of rejection. Instead, see it as the key to your financial freedom.

Go ahead. Take a swing. Give yourself the opportunity.

5
Hey-y-y-y!

Cool

Fear of rejection is nothing more than a thought. We choose our thoughts. We can choose to feel good or to feel bad when we get rejected.

Maybe you should feel bad when you get rejected. After all, look at what you did. You took the courage to act. And you tried to help someone else. Shame, shame, shame.

Rejection should be considered a Badge of Courage. Sales managers should reward those who collect the most rejections because they have the courage to make a difference.

If rejection bothers you, here are four techniques to deal with it.

The **President Jeb Bartlett technique**. One of my favorite TV shows was the now defunct *West Wing*. Often the president (Martin Sheen) was placed in difficult situations, but he and his staff did the best they could. Once the crisis was over, with his staff gathered around, he'd spread his arms, open the palms of his hands and say, "Ok. What's next?" He brought the situation to closure. Period. Over with. Move on.

Do the same thing when you're cold calling. When you get rejected, hang-up the phone, spread your arms, open the palms of your hands and say, "Ok. Who's next?" End that last call in your mind. Get your next dial tone and find someone else who's waiting for your help.

The **Find the Quarter technique**. Did you get rejected on that last call? Lose a customer because the competition came in at half your price? Didn't get picked for the company's softball team?

This is an easy way to deal with set-backs so they won't bother you again. Get a quarter. That's right, the good ole' American 25¢ piece. Look at the date and then find the mint mark (next to the date on newer quarters or under the eagle's tail feathers on older quarters) showing if the coin was made in Denver (D), San Francisco (S), or Philadelphia (no mint mark). You want to be able to recognize this quarter again later.

Now go outside and launch that Washington across the Delaware. Throw it down the street (watch out for cars!). Throw it into the bushes. Skip it across the lake. Just chunk it Plunkett.

That quarter represents your rejection. The only way you can be concerned about that rejection is to find that quarter and hold it in your hand again. If you can find it, worry and fret as much as you'd like. But if you can't find it, you can't be concerned because the problem is no longer yours.

What will you learn? It's not worth going after that quarter. Rejection's not worth two-bits after all.

The **Closer technique** is the quickest. Police Chief Will Pope on TNT's police series the *Closer*, tells a fellow officer whose feelings got hurt, "Take a minute…now get over it." Got too many other fish to fry.

Just Do It
Whatever advice you give, be short.
- Horace

Finally, use the **Fonz technique** and have fun with rejection. For those too young to remember, ABC used to air the comedy series *Happy Days*. You can still catch it on cable channels late at night. Henry Winkler played the character, the Fonz. He was the coolest guy in the gang. Everyone wanted to be the Fonz.

In the first year's shows, the credits rolled before the show began. As the credits passed over the Fonz (admiring himself in the mirror), and as the jukebox bopped Happy Days, the Fonz took out his comb, cautiously approached his lubricated hair, took a second admiring look, shrugged his shoulders, and put the comb back into his pocket. Why mess with perfection? Still mesmerized with himself in the mirror, he went two thumbs up with his cool trademark, "Hey-y-y-y!"

So the next time you get rejected, give them the Fonz. "Not interested." Hey-y-y-y. "Don't send a brochure." Hey-y-y-y. "Get off the phone you dirty, rotten, lousy cold caller!" Hey-y-y-y.

Don't believe it works? I'll prove it. Doctors have found that when you change your body language, you'll change your attitude faster than you can snap your fingers.

Take your thumb and hold it up. (Go ahead. No one's watching.) How do you feel? Positive? Now turn it down. How do you feel? Negative? Turn it up. Down. Up. Down. Up. Positive. Negative. Positive. Negative. Positive.

How long does it take to change your attitude? The flick of a wrist. Change your body language, change your attitude.

Fear of rejection. Never again let it stop you from calling to help others.

6

Coward

Semper Fi

The third cause of call reluctance is the lack of courage. Here's the first of two techniques that will give you the courage.

Dr. Viktor Frankl was an Austrian, a psychiatrist – and Jewish. At the beginning of World War II, he and his entire family were put into the German death camps. Dr. Frankl and his sister would be the only two to survive. At the end of the war he wrote the book, *Man's Search for Meaning*.

Dr. Frankl created the word logotherapy. He's also the father of the phrase *paradoxical intention*, which is what logothearpy means. His concept says that it seems the more you want something, the more elusive it becomes. The harder you try to grasp the prize, the more slippery it becomes. He said you can actually use this concept to your advantage, especially when it comes to physical sensations.

LOGOTHERAPY
(A.K.A. *Paradoxical Intention*)

"Happiness is like a butterfly. When pursued, always just out of reach. If one would sit quietly, it will come and light upon your shoulder." - - - Robert Louis Stevenson

For example, in the morning you're staring at that 300 pound phone, knowing you need to make your cold calls. Your hands begin to shake. Perspiration forms on your brow. Your breathing is rushed. Your voice squeaks. You surrender to your fears. You can't do it. You suddenly remember that report that's due next week. (Sales managers know that if they have paperwork that needs to be completed, just tell their salespeople to cold call.) You'll make your calls tomorrow.

No you won't. Who are you kidding?

Use Dr. Frankl's paradoxical intention to overcome your fears.

When you're cold calling, get a 3x5 card and write the word **COWARD** on it. Try to be a coward when you call the people. Try to physically shake. Try to hyperventilate. Try to have your mind go blank. The funny thing is, the harder you try, the calmer you get. Paradoxical intention.

An M.D.'s story

At the end of one of our Seattle seminars, I was approached by an attendee who was sitting on the front row. He pulled me to the side of the stage so no one else could hear what he was going to tell me.

He said, "Jerry, I'm an M.D., a medical doctor. My wife and I recently started a business on the side. It requires me to walk into businesses and drop off a brochure. A very simple type of cold call. But you know," he went on, "cold calling scares me. I don't like it."

He continued, "I'm going to try this coward thing and report back to you later what I think about it." I thanked him for his candor, and told him I'd appreciate his feedback.

Three months later, I got a very nice thank you card from the doctor. His note said, "You know, that coward thing really works! I don't know how or why it works but it works."

Dr. Frankl said the same thing. He said he never knew how the brain deals with paradoxical intention; it just does. And that's what I tell others. You don't have to know how it works, just use it.

Dr. Marty Nemko, the San Francisco business radio talk show host of *Work with Marty Nemko*, did an interview with me years ago and took the coward idea to a couple of friends.

"I've suggested it to two clients. The result? As Siskel and Ebert used to say, 'Two thumbs up.'"

And that's where we got the name of our seminars, Cold Calling for Cowards®. It's not that you are a coward, but if you try to be one, you'll find exactly the opposite happens. Paradoxical intention.

Exam day

You've used paradoxical intention all your life, but maybe you weren't aware of it. Think back to your high school or college days. You were required to take a certain course in order to graduate. It wasn't your favorite class, but you had to take it. Perhaps it was physics or chemistry or English.

Before the final exam you studied until you thought you'd puke. And you still couldn't "get it". Finally, out of desperation, you gave up. Threw your arms up in the air.

"There's no way I can pass this exam. I don't understand it. I'm going in tomorrow and I'm going to make the biggest, fattest 'F' this instructor has ever seen. I'll have to repeat this class again next semester."

Gud Luk

Commencement speaker's dilemma: "How can I tell the graduates that the future is in their hands without alarming the rest of the audience?"

- Unknown

And you quit studying. Maybe you went to a movie or went out for dinner the night before the big quiz. Everyone deserves a good last meal, right?

The next morning you walk into the exam room, relaxed, confident you'll fail. The exams are handed out. You stare at the questions in disbelief. It seems like they're the only ones you studied all year. You know the answers. You actually know the answers! It's a slam dunk. You ace the test.

What happened? Paradoxical intention. You tried to fail, but the exact opposite occurred.

The few, the proud

We were doing our seminar in Indianapolis. First thing in the morning, twelve U.S. Marines were the first group to arrive. They came in, full dress blues, ramrod straight, and the shortest Marine must have been 6'4". Proud Americans who make you proud by being in their presence. They sat on the front row.

Once the seminar got started, and before I explained the coward concept, I walked over to the edge of the stage, looked at one of the Gunnery Sergeants, and said, "Man – the name of this seminar must be *killing* you guys!" They and the audience laughed.

Once I explained the concept, they laughed even more. At the end of the program, the group of Marines told me they were recruiters. They said they had been using paradoxical intention all along without knowing what it was called or why it worked. I asked them to explain.

"In basic training, we get into the faces of the recruits. We call them every name in the book. We try to humiliate them. Demean them. We tell them they're mama's boys and they're not fit to wear the Marine blues. They'll wash out. They don't have what it takes. You're going to fail."

And then?

"And then they prove us wrong. They do exactly the opposite."
Semper fi.

7

Edgar Martinez

My, oh My!

The second technique to get the courage to call comes from the two-time American League batting champion Edgar Martinez.

The year is 1995. Seattle. The year that saved major league baseball in our city. Rumors had been flying that the team would be packing up for Tampa. Both Seattleites and players weren't happy about the prospect.

1995. The "Miracle Season". The first-ever year the Mariners made it to the playoffs. The Mariners tied the California Angels for first place in our division on the very last day of the season, leading to a one-game playoff for a berth to face the Evil Empire (a.k.a. New York Yankees) in the first round of the ALDS championship. Randy Johnson defeated Angel's ace Mark Langston 9-1. We took the next step.

The Mariners were trailing the Bronx Bombers two games to one in the best of five series. We had to win the next two at home to make it to the ALCS championship to face Cleveland.

October 7. Game four. Seattle's behind again. Edgar Martinez comes to the plate. Bases loaded. Edgar's already driven in three runs in the game. Does he have anything left? Is it in the cards? The pitch is on the way. He swings. He connects. It's – it's – the Grand Salami! Edgar wins the game and takes the team to the fifth and deciding game.

October 8. Kingdome. Electricity charges the sold out Cement Mushroom. Bottom of the 11th. Mariners down 5-4. This could be the end. Our shortstop little Joey Cora is the tying run on third. Ken Griffey, Jr., our ticket to the ALCS is on first. Coming to the plate…Edgar Martinez. The Yankees pitcher Jack McDowell is ready. The pitch is on the way. The swing. The crack. It's a screaming line drive down the third base line!

Cora scores easily from third to tie the game, guaranteeing a 12th inning to salvage the year. But Griffey has a different idea. The Kid takes off from first like a lightning bolt from Zeus at the swing of Edgar's bat. He rounds second. He's coming to third. Griffey has no intention of slowing down, regardless of the signs from the base coach. He rounds the bag wide heading for home. The ball arrives from the outfield like a bazooka to the catcher at the plate. He gloves it. The Kid slides.

He's SAFE! The Mariners win! The Mariners win! The Mariners win!

Every playoff season, the networks rebroadcast that famous photograph of Ken Griffey, Jr. being buried at home plate by his celebrating teammates. The famous Kid's smile at the bottom of the pile says it all. The kids from the West beat the men from the East in one of the most memorable playoff series in baseball history.

Cut away towards second base. Standing near second, with "The Double" as it's still known to Mariner fans today, is DH Edgar Martinez. Our hero again. He's being mobbed by the TV cameras and the media.

"Edgar!" someone shouts. "Were you trying to win the game? Were you trying to drive in Griffey?"

Relaxed, composed, and humble, Martinez explained his greatness.

"No man. I was just trying to make *contact* with the ball. The ball had to take care of itself."

And that's my second piece of advice to you when making your cold calls. Simply make contact with your prospects. Let the results take care of themselves.

You can control what you do. You can't control the results you get.

When you make contact, two things will happen. One: you'll get better on each call. Two: you'll improve your odds of finding new customers. Guaranteed.

Like Edgar Martinez, you've got to make contact to win.

Count on Me
Your future depends on many things,
but mostly on you.

- Frank Tyger

8

I Don't Have the Time
to Cold Call

Oops! Now You Do.

Conducting training with a group of traders at the Bank of America, their repeated excuse to their manager for not cold calling was, "I don't have the time. I'd like to – but man, I just don't have the time."

And He Doesn't Have a BlackBerry Either
The president of the United States has no more time than you.

- Unknown

I'm sure you've never used that excuse.

But there is some truth to it. Most salespeople don't have six to eight hours a day to spend cold calling. It's unreasonable. Even if you did, you'd burn yourself out. Besides, when are you going to have the time to sell? To follow-up? To put out the fires that spring up?

If time is an issue, here are two techniques that will help.

The **5-Minute technique**. Set aside five minutes of every hour to call. When the five minutes are up, take care of your normal business, sales calls, phone calls, and meetings. When the next hour arrives, call for five minutes again. The five minutes can come from any part of the hour. At the top of the hour. The bottom. The sides. Doesn't make any difference.

But – and this is critical – when your five minutes are up, stop calling. Make an agreement with yourself that you'll call for five minutes; but also agree that when your time is up you'll stop calling. You'll have a tendency to continue calling because you're "on a roll". But don't do it. You have to know that you can trust yourself to honor your self-commitments. I want you to get used to starting and stopping. The hardest part of calling is the starting part. But you need to get accustomed to starting several times throughout the day.

In five minutes, you'll make two, three, or four phone calls at the most. When the five minutes are up, stop calling and take care of your other business.

There are 244 working days per year. This allows for weekends, holidays, and vacation time. If you use the 5-Minute technique, you'll talk with over 5800 people this year. Now how hard is that?

"But," one of the traders told me, "I'm too busy to do even five minutes. You don't understand our business." I looked at the manager who pursed his lips and shook his head. Not true.

Okay. Let's go for the **3800/6 technique**. Every 30 minutes of every business day, give me one cold call. That's all. One cold call every 30 minutes. If you do this, you'll talk with over 3800 people this year that you've never talked with before. The 6? Each cold call shouldn't take more than 20-30 seconds. By doing one call every 30 minutes, you'll only take six minutes out of your day.

And if you still can't give me one call every 30 minutes, give me one call per hour. If you do this, you'll make over 1500 cold calls this year. That's probably 1400 more calls than you made all of last year.

I told the traders, "Tell me you don't like cold calling. Tell me it scares you. But never again tell me you don't have the time to do it, because I just showed you how."

9

Paradox of Cold Calling

Don't Try to Find Customers

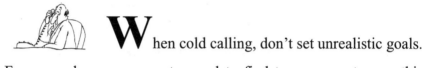**W**hen cold calling, don't set unrealistic goals. For example, you may set a goal to find ten new customers this month. The end of the month arrives and you've found two, maybe three, maybe none. You're discouraged. You failed to reach your goal.

As a result, when next month is ready to kick off, you're not. You set no new customer goals. You stop doing what it takes to fill the pipeline.

Step back. Take a deep breath. Return to goal setting basics. There are two types of goals you need to work.

Strategic goals. This is *what* you want. The results. (And remember, we can't control the results.) Is it two new customers this month? Three? Ten? How many new customers do your best salespeople find each month? That's your strategic goal.

Tactical goals. This is *how* you get what you want. These are the *activities* you can control and take. If you want to find three new customers this month, maybe you'll have to make twenty cold calls per day, send five direct mail pieces per day, and/or attend two chamber meetings this month.

And, yes, you'll get discouraged when you're calling. Maybe you won't find the number of new customers you want. Or find them fast enough. You're going to want to quit calling. How do you deal with jolts like this?

Simple. Don't call to find customers. Forget about it. Take the pressure off yourself.

How to Change a Lightbulb
Things do not change. We change.
- Henry David Thoreau

When calling, use the ***Paradox of Cold Calling***: instead of calling to *find* new customers, call to *eliminate* prospects.

Set a reachable goal of getting 20 rejections each day. Call and eliminate as many prospects as you can. Get them off your list. Get them out of your life. Get them outta' here. I don't know about you, but I can be rejected 20, 30, 40, or 50 times a day without breaking a sweat. But the crazy thing is, as I'm getting rejected, I start finding the customers. I'm taking the actions I need to take. But now there's no pressure. No failure. Only success.

A paradox.

Guaranteed: if you take the right activities, and keep improving those activities, you'll get the results you want. If you don't take the right activities, you'll never get the results that you want.

10

The Doctor Is In

Rx for Listening

One of the best pieces of advice I ever got was during my first year of selling. It was a two-page magazine advertisement (which shows you can learn anywhere, any time). One page, solid black, had this message:

> *LOOKING FOR THE SOLUTION WITHOUT LISTENING TO THE PROBLEM IS LIKE WORKING IN THE DARK.*

How would you like it if, when you go the doctor, you're sitting in the exam room and the doctor walks in, doesn't look at your chart, doesn't ask you any questions, and says, "Bud, you know we're going to have to amputate that left arm."

That's malpractice. He could be sued. Yet we as salespeople are guilty of doing the same thing. We get so excited about our service or product, we start pitching the features, advantages, and benefits, before finding out what the real problem is.

Listen to me. Listen to me. Listen to me. Customers are desperate for us to shut up and listen.

This is where women have it over the men. Let's say we've been given driving directions to the customer's office. We leave our office in Ft. Worth heading north on I-35 when we should be going south. Now men – we'll keep driving north until we get to Minneapolis before we ever ask for directions. At least women will stop and ask.

Research by Dr. Lillian Glass, *Talk to Win: Six Steps to A Successful Vocal Image*, shows that we spend 53% of our day listening, 50% of the people have hearing problems, and 50% of the message is lost by the untrained listener.

A Fortune 500 communications company asked me to go into the field with some of their representatives and observe their skills and techniques. At a customer's office the salesman took out his legal pad to take notes. Good. Shaking hands with the customer, the salesman put his legal pad on a side table and started asking questions. Bad.

After a couple of minutes of explaining his situation, the customer stopped in mid-sentence, looked squarely at the salesman, and said, "Hey! Aren't you taking notes? This is important to me."

***

Hang 10
Just as a wave is a manifestation of wind,
speech is the manifestation of thought.
- Rebecca Z. Shafir

***

Want to improve your listening skills? Use the **Golden Pad technique**. Get a legal pad. It's gold. Take notes. They'll make you gold. Did you know that when you take notes, you'll improve your retention by over 25%? You don't need to take any memory courses, don't need to read any of Harry Lorayne's great memory books. Simply take notes. Also, when you take notes, you're more likely to take action on what you've written down.

Even if you're reading a book, magazine, or newspaper article, it's been found that if you underline what's important to you, you'll increase your retention by one-third.

A business owner I know has a photographic memory, but she always takes notes when meeting with clients. I asked her why, since she can remember everything anyway.

"To show the customer I'm listening," she said. "To let her know it's important to me as well. Besides, if a conflict comes up later, I've got notes and she doesn't. When I refer back to them, the customer can't dispute her own words."

Listeners train speakers

You can also listen better with your arms. Robert Cialdini, author of *Influence: the Psychology of Persuasion*, reports on some experiments with college students. Groups of students were sent to lectures with specific instructions. Sit in your chairs, feet flat, arms uncrossed, chin up – don't take notes.

Other groups were then sent to the lectures. Sit in your chairs, cross your feet and arms, chin down, and don't take notes.

After the lectures, both groups were tested. The groups that went in, feet flat, arms uncrossed, and chin up scored 38% better than the groups that went in with arms and feet crossed. Plus, the students with their chins down were more negative and judgmental of the speaker.

Test this the next time you're talking with a co-worker. As your friend is speaking, cross your arms. During the same conversation, drop them. Cross them again. You'll notice that when your arms are crossed, not only are you blocking the speaker physically, you're also blocking him mentally.

When you're a good listener, you'll accomplish these three things: (1) you'll increase your influence with the speaker; (2) you'll develop quicker rapport; and (3) when it's your time to speak, you will have trained your customer to be a good listener for you.

So when you're cold calling on the phone, sit up, don't cross your feet, keep your chin up, and take notes. If you're doing walk-in cold calls, immediately after leaving the customer's office, take notes on the reverse of his business card. You'll remember better.

Are you listening?

11

The #1 Complaint of Customers

Why Men Can't Watch *The View*

 The #1 complaint of customers as found by Rebecca Z. Shafir, *The Zen of Listening?*

Interruptions.

Will you please stop interrupting me?!*

Body language experts Barbara and Allan Pease, *Why Men Don't Listen and Women Can't Read Maps: How We're Different and What to Do About It,* discovered some interesting things about us men. I told my wife that if their book wasn't so funny, it would be downright scary.

They found that men are competitive and aggressive in their conversations. Every word counts. Men are conversational bottom liners. Leave out the fluff, get to the point. And men hate being interrupted. They found that when two men are talking with each other, rarely will they interrupt one another. However, when men are talking with women, they're 76% more likely to interrupt the women.

Women are excellent multi-task conversationalists. Men are single-task talkers. That's why men can't watch *The View*. Their mind fogs over at the multiple conversations flying through the air and they become totally disoriented and dizzy. Yet the women hear every word, every nuance, every inflection. Drives men nuts.

The lesson for women in business? Even though it's not fair because they do it to you, don't interrupt men when they're talking. Be precise with your words. And get to the point with as few words as possible.

Shhhhh...
If you want to get people to listen, don't talk so much.

- Red Auerbach

How do you avoid the #1 complaint of interruptions? Use the **6 Second technique**. When you think the other party has finished speaking breathe in for two seconds. Hold your breath for two seconds. Breathe out for two seconds. And then speak.

The best place to practice this is with your family or co-workers. They'd love it if you'd stop interrupting them.

You don't need to use this technique every time, as many conversations are quick, spontaneous repartees. But the technique is especially useful when you're cold calling on the phone. You can't see the party at the other end of the line. Maybe someone has walked into her office and distracted her. Maybe she's lost her train of thought. Maybe she needs another gulp of O_2. Or maybe you asked a really good question and she's trying to form an appropriate answer.

If you interrupt her you may cause her to get off subject. You may provide an escape from a question that she didn't want to answer. By being courteous, you're also making yourself look good and buying yourself time to think on your feet.

Take a deep breath. Tell me what you think.

12

Would You Like Me to Wash That Brain for You?

Will You Need Bleach?

Remember in chapter one I asked you two silly questions, and then one question to test your honesty? Do you like to have fun? Are you open to new ideas? Wouldn't you really rather not have to cold call to find new customers? And I told you questions like those are important when you're cold calling.

Have you figured out why? To get your attention? They did, but that's not the reason. Because you should have fun when you're cold calling? Fun cold calling? I don't think so. You need to be open to new ideas? True, but still no cigar.

This is a Chinese brainwashing technique used on American P.O.W.'s during the Korean War. It's been around for thousands of years. Robert Cialdini, the Regents' Professor of Psychology at Arizona State University, published the research and coined the phrase *commitment and consistency* in his book *Influence: the Power of Persuasion* to refer to this phenomenon.

The concept is to *ask an easy, no-brainer question first* that the person knows the answer to without having to think, in order to get him to *go on record* with his answer; and then ask *progressively* more difficult and more difficult questions. When people go on record, rarely will they back down. They want to be consistent with each previous answer so they won't lose face. A small commitment gets them started. Consistency is the motivator that gets them to make larger concessions.

Don't shoot the messenger

Don't get upset with me and think I'm teaching you to manipulate others. I'm not. You don't. (But you do. You'll see.) I'm only the messenger. I'm trying to draw your attention to a principle that's been around for thousands of years so you'll know it when you see it.

You use this technique every day. It's used on you every day. You're just not aware of it. Once you become aware of it, you'll be able to help more people solve more problems.

Ever walk out of a company meeting, having volunteered to take on a project you know you don't have the time for, and wonder why you took it on? Commitment and consistency. Someone asked you the right questions, got you to go on record, and once you started agreeing, you couldn't back down.

Ever ask your teenager, "Now, you'll be home by 11. Right?" Who's manipulating whom?

It's in the DNA
My father had a profound influence on me—
he was a lunatic.

- Spike Milligan

When you took the morning off to wait for the cable guy, didn't you confirm it? "You'll be here before noon. Right? I'm taking off from work so I can be here."

The cable guy replied, "Sure. Around noon sometime."

That's not good enough. "No. When I made the appointment they said you'd be here before noon. I need to know – will you be here before noon or not?"

What about when you dropped the kids off at the grandparents for the night and bribed them with, "And if you're good we'll bring you a surprise." You started the technique on yourself.

"Really?" your child asks. He's strengthened the commitment.

"Really," you promise.

"Don't forget. You promised!"

How does your foot feel after your self-inflected wound?

Unconsciously, you're a master of commitment and consistency. But be careful with the questions you ask. Asking the wrong ones can work against you.

How about a test drive?

For example, you're looking for a new car. You're standing on the car lot and the salesman comes *sprinting* out of the showroom towards you. Not a good sign folks. Someone's not meeting quota.

"So-o-o," the salesman smiles as he slowly rubs his hands together, "what's it going to take to get you in this car today?"

You step back, showing him the palms of both hands, pushing away, "Hey…nothing. I'm just looking."

The salesman asked the right question, but at the wrong time. When asking qualifying questions, timing is everything. The prospect's gone on record as "just looking". It will be hard for him to back down on his answer without losing face. From now on, all his responses must be consistent with "just looking".

What would have been a better first question? Pick one. "Ever owned a car before?" "Is that your car over there?" "Been looking long?" "See my office door over there? Here's my card. If you have any questions, please come and get me."

Running with the bulls

They did some research on commitment and consistency with some brokers in Los Angeles. They were to make their cold calls from a list given to them by their sales manager. The second question they were to ask: "Do you have $10,000 you'd like to invest?"

They made their calls. I'm sure they heard answers like these. "$10,000? That's none of your business." "Invest? I never invest." "$10,000 to invest? Are you nuts?"

They made several hundred calls and didn't get a single appointment. The next day the sales manager put the brokers in their cars and drove through the territory they were calling. Beverly Hills. Bel Air. These people don't have $10,000? These people don't invest?

Right question. Wrong sequence.

They went back to their office and re-positioned the $10,000 question as question number six. They started calling again. They got appointments that led to sales. Timing is everything.

Wrapped around her little finger

Here's how it's used in your personal life. Daphne, our oldest daughter, got her driver's license in high school. She came to me the day she got it and asked, "Dad, can I borrow the car for the game Friday night?"

An easy, no-brainer question. I knew the answer to this one. Plus, I was expecting it.

"Sure no problem."

She came to me the next day, rubbing her finger tips together. "Dad, do you have ten bucks I can borrow for gas? I don't have any money."

Being a concerned parent, I took out my wallet. Don't want her to get stranded in the middle of the night somewhere.

Two days later, the day of the game, she came to me again, "Dad, I know my curfew is at 11:30. But you know, this is homecoming. Could I stay out until 1?"

What was she doing to me? That's right. She was setting me up. She was using commitment and consistency. I fell for it. And I teach it!

---

*Are You Nuts!?**
It helps if the hitter thinks you're a little crazy.

- Nolan Ryan

Homework

Your homework: develop seven qualifying questions you'd like to ask every prospect on every cold call and then number them in sequence, the easiest to the most difficult. The money question will usually be one of the last questions.

Why seven questions? Based upon research by Bell Laboratories years ago, they found that people can remember, do, and respond to things in a sequence of seven. That's why they made phone numbers seven digits long.

Here are three examples of *bad* first questions to ask.

"How about an appointment?" That's a good question to ask, but not a good first question. People don't like to be put on the spot that quickly and will become defensive.

"How much money do you want to spend?" Again, a good question, but not a good first question.

"Who's *really* the decision-maker in your family?" Wives love that one. Ask that and kiss your commission check bye-bye.

Qualifying questions reveal clues

Here are seven qualifying questions I'd ask if I sold banking services.

1. "Do you have a commercial account with any other banks?" That's an easy, no-brainer question. They know the answer. Even you know the answer before you ask it. But here's the thing: even if you know the answer, don't assume it's the right answer and don't state it like a fact. Ask it as a question to get them to respond and to go on record to start the commitment and consistency technique.

2. "How long have you been with them?" They'll have to think on this a little. When you get your answer, it's a good indicator of their loyalty to your competitor. And sometimes they may even make a statement like, "You know, we've been thinking of looking around, but we've been putting it off."

3. "What kinds of accounts do you have: deposit, loans, real estate?" This question gets them to think a little more about their needs. It may reveal that they may have a line of credit with one bank, a real estate loan with another. This also indicates that they're willing to do business with multiple banks.

4. "Do you have any needs for business insurance or CD's?" Notice the questions are getting a little more difficult.

5. "What's the most important thing you look for from your bank?" If they answer this, it shows interest in you. Make a note of what they say, because this could get you the business down the road.

6. "Is your company growing to a stage where we could *compete* for any of your business?" I discovered that one word *compete* is important in banking. A top-level decision-maker banker who attended our seminar in Baltimore told me during the break that his bankers/salespeople get a ton of appointments by using that one word. "Why?" I asked. "Because many people still don't realize that banks can compete and negotiate with rates. They think banks and rates are locked in."

7. "If I promise to not take more than 15 minutes of your time, either on the phone or in person, could I make an appointment and ask you a few more questions about your business and goals? I don't want to do a presentation since we don't know enough about each other yet." This question accomplishes two things. First, I let the prospect know that I won't take more than 15 minutes. We both know that we can qualify or disqualify each other this quickly. Second, I'm not going to do a show and tell. I want to learn more

about his business and goals so I'll know if we're a fit.

I can usually disqualify someone within two or three questions. If you disqualify them, or they disqualify you this quickly, forget the other questions and move on. However, if you make it through all seven qualifying questions, you may have a good suspect (not a prospect yet) on the line. The appointment will determine if he's a prospect later.

Knowing how to ask the right questions at the right time is one of the most powerful techniques in cold calling and selling. The better you qualify someone, the more deals you'll close. Every question must serve one, if not two, purposes. In today's business world, time is the most precious commodity people can give you. Don't abuse it. Don't wing it. This may be your only shot.

Throughout the book, I'll show you several more ways the commitment and consistency technique is used.

13

How to Think on Your Feet Faster

You Couldn't Buy a Better List of Prospects

Cold calling reveals three levels of prospects every time. The reason this is important to know is because you'll be prepared and be two steps ahead of the prospects. Since you know they're going to respond one of three ways, you'll be ready with your follow-up questions.

Let's say you compile a list of names from the Internet or rip out the Yellow Pages and start calling at random. You have no history on the prospects.

Your first call may be to a **Level 1 prospect**. Level 1 uses your service or product from your company already. Turns out, they're an existing customer and you didn't know it. Most new salespeople with their company try to convince the sales manager they don't want to start cold calling until they memorize their customer database. They don't want to embarrass themselves. They're not fooling anyone. They don't want to cold call, period.

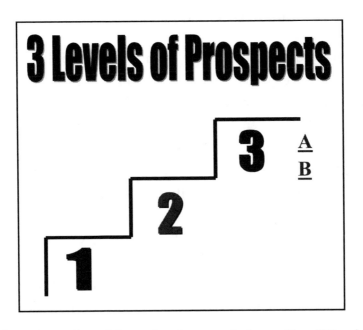

If you get a Level 1 on the phone and she replies, "You know, we're a customer with your company already," don't panic. Calmly reply, "Oh, great. How's our service? How's our billing? Should I have your sales rep contact you?" Then hang-up and make your next call.

Your second call may be to a **Level 2 prospect**. Level 2's use your service or product from your competitor. These people will determine your success in selling. We'll come back to them later.

Your third call may be to a **Level 3 prospect**. A Level 3 does not use your service or product. Not from you. Not from your competitor. Level 3's have two sub-levels: A and B. Sub-level 3A has no intention of ever using your service or product. Not now. Not in the future. Sub-level 3B may be thinking about using what you sell within the next three to six months.

Would you like to be converted?

You make a decision on the 3A's: do you want to do missionary work with these people? Or not? Do you want to convert these people? Or do you want to move on?

For example, when we were selling cellular phones when they first came out in the mid-80's, we were dealing with the 3A's. No one had cell phones so they had to be sold on the concept – educated – as to how words could fly through the air and reach their phone as they're driving 60 m.p.h. down the freeway. We even went into great detail as to how the cell towers were designed and worked.

Cell phone's pioneering legend Craig McCaw, our boss, told us that when you're selling a service or product in its concept stage it's going to be a longer sell. As a result the commissions will be higher. (We were making commissions of $200-$500 per phone. Of course, customers were paying $1 per minute for talk time.) But he warned us that once cell phones became a retail product – where people can walk into the store and buy them off the shelf – the commissions would disappear and the caliber of salespeople required to sell concepts would no longer be required. (Salespeople are lucky to get $15 per phone today.)

Selling to 3A's will be a longer selling cycle, but the rewards will be greater.

3B prospects are quicker sales. They understand the concept of what you're selling. Maybe their friends have one. Or they've seen it advertised on TV. They're the late bloomers, the procrastinators. These are the last people to buy the BlackBerrys or iPods or Bluetooths. Pre-need funeral consultants tell me they never schedule appointments with anyone younger than 30 because they don't think they'll die. But…things change.

There's gold in them thar Level 2's

Let's return to Level 2's. They have something you want. They have a problem. You know this because they're using your competitor's solution. (That's your problem.)

But this is guaranteed: things change. Decision-makers come and go. Needs come and go. Money comes and goes. And competitors come and go.

Waiting is a Skill
In an ambush situation, waiting is what wins the battle. You need infinite patience. No use fretting or worrying. You just wait. Doing nothing, thinking nothing, burning no energy. Waiting is a skill like anything else.

- Lee Child
Author of Jack Reacher mystery novels

Harvey Mackay, *Dig Your Well Before You're Thirsty* and *Swim with the Sharks without Being Eaten Alive*, said that when things change, make sure you've positioned yourself to be the #2 vendor on the prospect's list so you'll be the first person they call. Because when things change, and they will, they're not calling #3, #4, or #5. They're only calling #2. (See *Appendix B* "Positioning Yourself to Be #2 – Making the Short List Without Becoming a Pest" for how to get prospects to call you first.)

Not only do Level 2's have a problem, they have money budgeted to take care of it. They make quicker decisions. They don't need committees. They understand what you're selling.

Earlier, I mentioned the author who said cold calling doesn't work because people (Level 2's) already have what you're selling. His inference is that they only buy once and will never buy again. But things change. I'm excited to see people doing business with my competitor. They've been educated, they have the budget, and they have the need. No committees. Quick decisions.

According to a Bain & Co. study published in the *Harvard Business Review*, U.S. companies lose 50% of their customers every five years. And one of the contributing factors: salespeople lose contact with their customers. If you have five, six, or seven competitors and each loses 50% of his customers every five years, wouldn't you be excited too? (See ***Appendix C*** "Increasing Customer Retention – It's About Staying Connected" for a proven customer retention program that can be yours.)

Convert these stats into sales

Knowing these statistics isn't enough. You have to convert this knowledge into sales. When cold calling you must do these three things to increase your income:

First, cold call to **identify** who the prospects are in your territory – *and* **who** they're doing business with. Forget about trying to sell them on the first call. It's not going to happen. Call and identify is the order of the day.

Second, **keep records** on every customer and prospect you call on. Get a good customer relationship management (CRM) software program like ACT! (sign-up for free 30-day trial at www.act.com/trial). By keeping records, you will eliminate 80% of your competitors who are too lazy. Here's what I mean.

Consolidated Freightways was a 73-year old national trucking company based in Vancouver, Washington. On Labor Day 2002, they declared bankruptcy and locked their gates. If I was their competitor, I would have been religiously cold calling my territory and I would have known who every one of their customers were. I would have been on the phone that Tuesday morning calling their orphaned customers. Customers with shipments sitting on the docks going nowhere.

I picked up dozens of new accounts doing the same thing at McCaw Communications. Competitors came and went in the volatile communications business almost on a quarterly basis. Their salespeople didn't have the stick-to-itiveness. Plus, their customers' decision-makers changed regularly. When things changed, and because I had a list of all prospects in my territory and who they were doing business with, I could be on the phone and in the door of my new customers before my competitors could devise a strategy.

Say "cheese!"

I learned the importance of identifying prospects and keeping records in my first sales job. Selling for Jackson, Mississippi, based School Pictures, Inc., the world's largest school picture company at the time, it was ingrained in me that people do business with people – not with companies. That's when I learned that when a salesperson/photographer left the business, his principals' loyalties left with him. As a result, because I knew who the principals and their photographers were, and because I kept in touch, I picked up new business quickly.

Mr. Smith (his real name) a principal of an elementary school in my territory told me that he was loyal to Mr. Wheat, my competitor. They had been good friends for over 20 years. I liked Mr.

Wheat, too, since he had taken my senior picture in high school. I told Mr. Smith I appreciated his loyalty and would respect it.

"But," I asked, "could I position myself to be the #2 photographer on your list – just in case anything happens? Could I drop by from time to time to say hi? I promise I'll never ask you for your business, but if you ever get ready to change, I'd like to be the first person you call."

"No problem," Mr. Smith said.

I kept in touch for the next couple of years. One summer day I read Mr. Wheat's obituary in the paper. I was sorry to see his passing. But I wasn't going to rush over to Mr. Smith's school. He said he'd call me first if he ever changed. I trusted him.

Two weeks passed. No call. Three weeks. Six. Still no word from Mr. Smith. School started in September. The month was almost gone. Schools like to have their pictures made early in the year so they can get them back before the Thanksgiving break. Mr. Smith was cutting it close. Did he forget me? Did he decide to go with someone else?

I stopped by his school. "Mr. Smith, have you scheduled your fall pictures yet?" I asked, dreading to hear that he may have given the business to another photographer.

"No, Jerry, I haven't," he replied. "I'm still waiting for Mr. Wheat to give me a call."

Oh.

How could I bring it up?

"Uh, Mr. Smith. I didn't come here to tell you this. I thought you already knew. I'm sorry you have to hear it from me. But Mr. Wheat passed away this summer."

Mr. Smith was surprised. "No. No, I didn't. I'm sorry to hear that. He was a good man."

"Yes he was."

I felt awkward being the bearer of bad news. I got up to leave. "I'm sorry to have brought the bad news. Tell you what, if you don't mind I'll stop by in a couple of weeks and we can talk again." I didn't want to ask for the business and take advantage of a delicate situation.

"Oh, no, no Jerry. Have a seat. Let's set a date for our pictures. I promised if I ever changed photographers, I'd do business with you."

I had Mr. Smith's friendship and business until I left the industry.

I did something accidentally in this selling process I wasn't aware of until years later. Maybe you missed it too. I used the principle of commitment and consistency. I got Mr. Smith to go on record that he would do business with me if anything ever changed. He committed. By keeping in touch, I applied consistency. Every time I stopped by he'd say something like, "Well, things still haven't changed. Mr. Wheat is still doing my pictures. But if they change, I'll be sure to call."

How to eliminate 95% of your competitors

The third thing you need to do when cold calling: **keep in touch**. If you keep in touch, you'll be ahead of 95% of your competitors. Only 5% of salespeople keep in touch with their customers and prospects. It's the only way to position yourself to be #2 and make the short list.

Salespeople don't keep in touch because they're lazy, they don't know how to do it, or they're afraid they'll come across as a pest. They want to be persistent, yet don't want to be seen as a stalker.

Couldn't buy a better list

Finally, look at what you're doing by cold calling, keeping records, and keeping in touch. You can take the worst list you have and create the best list you'd ever want. You couldn't buy a better collection of names from a list broker than the one you create from cold calling. Because you're keeping records on your prospects, you have the names of decision-makers, influencers, names of their vendors, what they're buying, how much they're paying, and how often they're buying. There's no better list than this.

How valuable is this list? What if your competitors had a copy of your list? What would they do with it? Speaking from experience, if your competitors know you have a list like this, and they know you're leaving the industry, they'll pay you a lot of money for it. Offers have been made to me, but out of respect for my previous employers I have never turned the names over. But that shows how valuable those names can be.

And look how you got them. By cold calling.

Need I Say More?
I do want to get rich but I never want to do what there is to do to get rich.
- Gertrude Stein

14

Listen Up!

Gatekeepers Are Giving Clues

When cold calling, listen for any of these five clues from the mouths of gatekeepers:

1. The company's undergoing change.
2. There's new management.
3. The company's reorganizing.
4. The company's consolidating resources.
5. There's a merger.

These clues indicate two principles are at work within the organization: (a) the company is spending money freely; and (b) they're making decisions quickly.

If the gatekeeper says, "Sorry, we're not interested at this time. We just hired a new general manager and we're not looking to make any more new changes," she doesn't understand the concept of a new general manager.

As I'm writing this, Alan Mulally has left our Seattle Boeing Commercial Airplane Company to take over as CEO of the Ford Motor Company. In this, just his first week, he has announced the offer to buy-out all 75,000 hourly union members and the projected layoff of 14,000 white collar salaried workers.

Not looking to make any more changes? Surprise!

That manager has been brought in to make changes, and make them today. And chances are he's got the money in the budget, and decisions will be made quickly without going through committees. And rarely will he go to bid. He may talk with two, maybe three competitors at most. Plus, to show his independence and break from the past, he will probably fire many of the current vendors to prove he can do it, and bring his own vendors on board.

Hope you've been keeping in touch with your customers so they'll take you with them.

15

In the Blink of an Eye

Snorkeling with Socrates

Customers buy into three things before they would ever consider buying your service or product.

The first thing the customer buys: **you**. Unless you have a monopoly on what you sell, if she doesn't like you, she'll go to your competitor. However, if she likes you and trusts you, and even though you may have a higher price or inferior product or service, she'll still buy from you because of the relationship.

Malcolm Gladwell, sociologist and author of the 2005 *New York Times* best seller *Blink*, often referred to research from Harvard psychologist and Professor Dr. Nalini Ambady that found people are making accurate decisions about you in less than two seconds. Dr. Ambady said "you better master the first few seconds".

Two seconds? Scrap that. In the July 2006 issue of the journal *Psychological Science*, Princeton University assistant professor of psychology Alex Todorov and his co-author Janine Willis found that people are making accurate judgments about your "attractive-ness, likeability, trustworthiness, competence, and aggressiveness" in *one-tenth of a second*. The power of first impressions.

Additional research found that 71% of the purchasing decision is based upon *trust* between the salesperson and the prospect. So the first thing people buy is you.

Fright smile

The second thing people buy: **benefits or opportunities**. "What's in it for me? How will it make my life better? Easier?"

Imagine you're the sales manager of a company that recently hired five new salespeople to cold call on the telephone. How would you sell them on the benefits of smiling on the phone? After all, no one can see them. What's in it for them?

Well, for one thing, it makes you feel better. And if you feel better, it comes across in your tone and voice.

You'll be more enthusiastic. You can actually convey your en-thusiasm through the telephone.

It relaxes you. If you're relaxed, the person at the other end won't tense up.

Smiling changes your attitude. It creates the law of attraction. If you go to work with that sourpuss face, how many people will enjoy hanging out with you?

Smiling helps you to listen better. Smiling makes you more open and receptive.

People mirror smiles. Even though you're on the phone, people can tell if you're angry, upset, or smiling. Their tone and voice will reflect back to you exactly what they hear. That's why good cus-tomer service people are invaluable. They can take an angry caller, and with the smile in their voice, quickly convert him from the dark side.

Finally, smile for medical reasons. Doctors have found that when you smile – even if it's a forced smile – it releases endorphins into the brain. Endorphins fight stress. Doctors say these endorphins are twenty times more powerful than morphine.

One of our seminar attendees said that all her salespeople are required to keep a mirror on the wall of their cubicles above the phone. Across the top of the mirror is written, "The person you see is the person they hear."

If you have to cold call – if it's going to be scary…well then, you might as well smile about it.

What was Socrates selling?

To explain the third thing people buy into, see if you can guess what Socrates was selling. If you can, then you'll understand what affects 70% of your buyers and how to influence their decisions.

A young man approached the Greek scholar. "Socrates," he asked, "when will I have all the knowledge I need?"

Some People Never Learn
Experience is a hard teacher. She gives the test first, the lesson afterwards.
- Unknown

Without saying a word, Socrates took the young man into the river, waded out about waist high, grabbed the man by the back of the neck, and shoved his head under the water. The man didn't have to be a genius to understand that he was about to drown. He began fighting and clawing and finally got his head above the water to breathe life again.

Socrates looked at the terrified man and shrugged his shoulders. "Son," the wise teacher said, "when you want knowledge as badly as you wanted that air, then you will have it."

My question to you: what was Socrates really selling? If you can understand what Socrates was selling, then you'll understand what 70% of your prospects are buying into.

Knowledge? No, he created knowledge because of what he was selling.

Opportunity? No, he created opportunity because of what he was selling.

Trust? I don't think so. I'd never trust him again after a stunt like that.

What Socrates was selling, and what 70% of your prospects are buying into: the **problem**.

"Son, *you've* got a problem. *You* can't breathe. What are *you* going to do about it?"

Notice that Socrates didn't have to do any fancy closes. "Son, would you rather breathe on Tuesday, or does Thursday work best for you?" Never came up.

Socrates didn't have to use the Benjamin Franklin close: "Now these are the advantages of breathing, and these are the disadvantages of not breathing." This never came up because the young man was immersed in the problem.

70% of the people you call on are trying to avoid problems. Only 30% are looking for benefits and opportunities.

Life preserver to follow

Certain sales personalities always begin their questioning with a statement like this: "If I could show you a way to take advantage of this exciting new opportunity, wouldn't you be interested?" These poor salespeople don't understand that they have a 7 in 10 chance they're talking with someone who could care less about opportunities.

If you don't know who these 70% and 30% are when cold calling, you must talk about both problems and opportunities during the call. But later in the book you'll be given one question that quickly identifies which is which.

That question may save you from drowning.

16

Did I Say That?

Don't Commit Vocal Suicide

Do prospects detect the fear in your voice? Do you come across as unsure and timid? Does your voice betray you? Where – exactly – do you give away your confidence when cold calling and how can you get it back?

The sound and tone of your voice account for 38% of your message. The words themselves only 7%. How you look when you say what you're saying accounts for the other 55%.

Try the simple exercise on the next page to create confidence in your voice. Write out the script you want to deliver on your cold call. Then draw an arrow at the end of each sentence to see if your voice rises or falls.

For example, my first reading of the script may go something like this:

"Hi?" Because I'm nervous, my greeting sounds like a question. The voice rises. I draw an up arrow.

"This is Jerry Hocutt with You've Got Contacts?" My voice rises again. I've still got the jitters. Another up arrow.

I've given away my confidence in the first two lines – the easiest lines of all. And that's where people commit vocal suicide. The first two lines. It doesn't sound like I'm even sure of who I am. I need to be more definite. Instead of raising my voice, I should be dropping it. Like planting a flag.

Hi ⇧⬇

This is Jerry Hocutt with You've Got Contacts ⇧⬇

I'd like to give your company two free sales tools to help increase your sales ➡

I was calling to see...who could I send some information to at your company about this free service ⬆

Here's how the call should sound.

"Hi!" Exclamation point. Arrow down.

"This is Jerry Hocutt with You've Got Contacts!" No doubt about it. I know who I am. Down arrow.

"I'd like to give your company two free sales tools to help increase your sales." Here the voice may stay even. Horizontal arrow.

"I was calling to see (pause) who could I send some information to at your company about our service?" Now the voice rises; it's a question. Arrow up.

Listen to the people in your office when they make their first cold calls of the day. Or any call that scares them. Maybe it's a complaint they're responding to. Maybe the customer's product is delayed. Maybe they're calling to get a payment. But listen to their opening lines. Almost always they've lost their confidence on the easiest lines of all.

How do you limber up your voice and get it into gear before making those scary calls? That's our next lesson.

17

Monster Truck
Extravaganza Voice

Go for It!

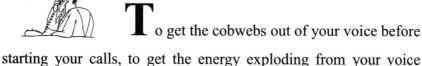**T**o get the cobwebs out of your voice before starting your calls, to get the energy exploding from your voice like an awakened Mt. St. Helens, use your **WWE SMACKDOWN** announcer's voice when driving in to work each morning.

Make the macho **MONSTER TRUCK EXTRAVAGANZA** guy envious of your down and dirty, throaty, guttural delivery as you read the signs along the highway.

STOP!
yield right of way

Express Lanes Open **Open Open**

Yield to oncoming traffic

No Turn on Red **Never Nada** Don't do it!

SPEED LIMIT 55!!!!!

Change your rate of delivery. Change your inflections. Pause. Pause often. When you pause, it gives the listener the chance to catch up with you. It gives you a chance to catch your breath. And when you pause you...put...emphasis...on...what...you're...saying.

But make sure that when doing this exercise, you're in the car by yourself. If you're carpooling, the others may think you're a little weird. If you're on the L in the Big Apple or the Windy City, they'll be putting you off at the next stop.

Lighten up. Make it fun. What'll others do? Laugh? Good. They deserve to feel better too.

18

Not Fair But True

Don't Let Your Voice Give You Away

 The following statement is not fair – but true.
People who have a deeper voice are perceived as having more authority. Not fair. But true.

Darth Vader of Star Wars fame. Remember that rich, deep, ominous voice? Who was the voice of Darth Vader? That's right. James Earl Jones.

We were doing our seminar in Detroit and I asked the group, "Who does James Earl Jones sound like to you?"

A lady in the far back of the room yelled out, "God!"

I laughed with the audience. If God has a voice, that's the voice I want to hear.

Now picture this: Darth Vader. This villain is scary looking. Black caped uniform. Intimidating mask for a face. Rasping breaths. But this time imagine the high-pitched, whinny voice of Megan Mullally (who played Karen on *Will & Grace*) coming out of that face. Would he have the same affect? Not even close.

If people with deeper voices are perceived as being authoritative, yet you have the annoying voice of a Gilbert Godfried or the fingernails-on-the-chalkboard screech of a Roseanne Barr, what can you do? Drop it several octaves until you reach the George Clooney or Julia Roberts range? I wouldn't recommend it. You could damage your vocal chords and ruin your voice if you try to make any radical changes.

CSI
Little clues lead to big discoveries.
- Gil Grissom

The secret

Instead, when you're calling on the phone, stand up. When you stand up, you change the energy level throughout your body immediately. You change your attitude. Both feet are firmly planted on the floor giving you a grounded, secure feeling. And then, this is the secret, place all of your weight on one foot. Try to drive your foot through the floor as hard as you can. (But keep both feet on the ground! Just shift your weight to one foot.)

You'll notice that your voice drops one octave without straining your vocal chords. Your voice sounds richer and fuller. More confident.

To prove this, when you're in your car and driving to your next appointment or driving home tonight, count to ten in your normal tone of voice: 1 – 2 – 3 – 4 – 5 – 6 – 7 – 8 – 9 – 10.

Now, press your foot through the floorboard as hard as you can and count to ten again. (But which foot? Your left foot! I know it's more thrilling to press down with your right foot, but please don't.)

Compare the difference. You'll notice that your voice sounds deeper, richer, and fuller.

But what can you do in a meeting when you can't stand up? What if you know you're about to be called on and you're afraid your butterflies will give you away? Simply grab the bottom of your chair with one hand (they won't notice what you're doing) and pull up as you respond. It's like the Isometric exercises you can do at your desk. This has the same effect as pressing your foot.

One final note to instill confidence. Maybe you're preparing to cold call, or call to ask a customer why he hasn't paid his bill, or get up in front of the room to give a sales presentation. If you're nervous, stand up for about 30 seconds with your hands behind your back (what's known as the palm-in-palm gesture) and raise your chin. You don't need to say or do anything else. The butterflies begin to leave. Confidence is restored. Body language calms if the mind shakes.

19

One Ring-y Ding-y

The Dork Factor

 Is it better to use a telephone handset or headset when calling?

Let's consider the handset first. Most right-handed people will put the receiver on their left ear so they can write with their right hand. Left-handed people do the opposite. But look what happens to your body.

Cradling the phone between your ear and shoulder all day will have you driving home at night with a permanent tilt to your head, hunch in your shoulders. You'll be wondering, "Why does my neck hurt so much?"

At the same time your chin covers the mouthpiece. Your voice sounds mumbled. Also, your chin is down. When your chin is down, you speak in a monotone and have a negative attitude. Your neck is stiff, your shoulders are stiff, and your voice is tense.

Now compare using the telephone headset. Only 10% of people use headsets. (More people are beginning to use them with their cell phones and, of course, Bluetooths.) The reason people don't like using headsets is what I call the **Dork Factor**. I look like a dork. I feel like a dork. Therefore, I must be a dork.

The Latest Buzz
Does that noise in my head bother you?
- Narrator
The Gods Must Be Crazy

But once you get over this sensation, you'll never go back to a handset again. By getting a good wireless headset, you have the ability to stand up and move around. I prefer both the Plantronics wireless and GN Netcom wireless and use both in our offices. Plus, a headset allows you to use your arms, hands, and body language when talking. Using a headset allows you to keep your chin up and put inflections in your voice. You'll sound like you're talking *with* someone instead of *into* something.

With the handset, you're also putting the receiver on the wrong ear. Right-handed people should put the receiver on their right ear; left-handed people on their left. Headsets allow you to do this, leaving your writing hand free for taking notes.

Why is the correct ear important? Based upon research by Dr. Alfred Tomatis, a French ear, nose, and throat specialist, the brain will save one-tenth to two-tenths of a second in processing words from the right ear to the left brain (the language side of the brain for right-handed people). The opposite applies to left-handers. Dr. Tomatis said this is enough time to put the words into the correct sequence to listen better and learn faster. Using his Tomatis Methods through over 250 clinics worldwide, he has helped thousands of people deal with their problems with dyslexia, ADD, and learning disabilities because they learn how to listen better.

Stick a fork in the Dork. He's done.

20

Shooting from the Lip

You've Got 20 Seconds

Should you use a script when cold calling? Do actors? Does the President when giving his State of the Union? Does your minister, priest, or rabbi use prepared notes?

Then what makes you so special that you can shoot from the lip?

I'm not a believer in a script that you write out and read or that you memorize. That's why you won't see any scripts presented in this book. What you'd say and what I'd say are two different things. If I were to write your script, you wouldn't deliver it with any sincerity. Besides, even each call is different.

That's a Nasty Slice
Most mistakes are made before the club is swung.

- Harvey Penick

But I also don't believe in being completely spontaneous. You wouldn't think of doing improv at the Comedy Club would you? You'd bomb. Yet, by trying to wing our cold calls we're cluster bombing – and it costs us in embarrassment, time, and money. One reason cold calls explode in our faces, the reason people would rather die than give a speech, is because of the lack of preparation. Even those who are paid to do improv prepare.

One problem with being spontaneous is that today you might be having a good day; tomorrow you're having a lousy day. Why? You could have changed one word or phrase in your delivery and you've changed the results you're getting. And if nothing is written down, you don't know what is and isn't working.

But there is a compromise between reading a script and winging it. It's called being extemporaneous – you sound like you're spontaneous, but you know exactly where you're going with the program. You have a starting point. An ending point. And you allow for bumps along the way.

An extemporaneous script is like a surgeon performing an appendectomy. You know where to cut, what you're looking for, how to suture, and what to do if things start going south. You've got a game plan, but you leave enough versatility in your approach to allow for adapting to a variety of scenarios.

It's your baby – love it

You must own your script. Don't let someone else write it for you. Take their ideas, cover all their points, but the words have to be yours. Otherwise, you'll be like those salespeople you hang-up on before they spit out, "Hi, Ms. Roberts. How are y…?" Click.

Your scripts use the words you use in the way you'd deliver them. If I were to write a script for you, you'd look at it in disgust. That's not the way you talk. That sounds so hokey. Screw that.

Write your own script. Then re-write, re-write, and re-write it until it sounds like you. After you think you have it down, read through it multiple times – out loud. You'll find that how you speak is not how you write. Once you rehearse your script enough to know it backwards and forwards you can deliver it without ever having to look at it.

Scripts for cold calling are especially important. Because you're in a tense situation, your mind sometimes goes blank. You're likely to ramble. You'll get tongue-tied. But a good script allows you to be concise and effective in your delivery.

No cold call script should be more than 30 seconds long; 20 seconds is ideal. One minute is suicide. You need a script because it allows you to cover all your main points while staying on point. A good script gives you confidence that's reflected in your voice.

It's a hit!

When you hang-up the phone, how will you know you've delivered a successful script? Before you create your script, write down your objectives. If you hit half of them on each call, you've got a good script.

I have seven objectives:

1. Start a relationship.
2. Get the decision-maker's name.
3. Qualify or disqualify the prospect.
4. Maintain my composure.

5. Create frequency of contact.
6. Keep the initiative so I can call back.
7. Improve my techniques.

Using the script below I can get the decision-maker's name 95% of the time. I immediately qualify or disqualify the prospect. He can do the same to me. Because I'm using my own words, and because I've rehearsed them until they're a part of me, I'm not rattled by the situation.

Inquiring Minds Want to Know
Are you worth talking to for the next ten minutes?

- Peggy Klaus

I create the opportunity to stay connected after this call. The script sets the prospect up for two more contacts. This call, coupled with the two follow-ups (sending the information and then calling back to see if they've received it) makes three contacts with the prospect. Psychologists have found that people have to see you, see your name, or hear your name six times before they will trust you enough to buy. I'm half-way home.

Finally, after every call, I evaluate what happened so I can improve my next call. Like a batter in the big leagues, I'm trying to improve my average.

Here's my cold call script from chapter 16. Look it over, and then we'll analyze it.

> *Hi. This is Jerry Hocutt with You've Got Contacts. I'd like to give your company two free*

*sales tools to help increase your sales. I was
calling to see…who could I send some information to at your company about this free service?*

Don't blow it

What I've achieved with an extemporaneous script:

a. I can deliver my message in 10 seconds. The script works
   with anyone who answers the phone: gatekeeper, influen-
   cer, or decision-maker.

b. I start building trust by giving them my full name. On the
   phone, people are more suspicious if you don't give them
   your name or only give them your first name. Don't worry.
   They won't remember it anyway. If they're interested,
   they'll ask for it again. And don't try to come across as if
   you're good buddies who go way back. This may buy you a
   few extra seconds, but when they figure out you were trying to deceive them, you've lost trust.

c. I create credibility by giving them my company name. This
   makes me look legitimate. They're thinking someone trusted you enough to hire you, maybe I can trust you for a few
   more seconds to hear what you have to say.

d. I was direct and I told them what I want. "I'd like to give
   your company two free sales tools to help increase your
   sales." People hate it when you beat around the bush. Get
   to the point. I've also achieved extra leverage by making
   two value statements in this sentence. One: I want to give
   them something free. Two: I know every company, every

business owner, every sales manager needs to increase his sales, so I'm speaking to a real need.

e. I tell them what I want them to do: volunteer the name of their decision-maker. And when I ask for the name, I use a magic word to improve my odds for getting it. I ask, "...who could I *send* some information to...?" *Send* works magic. By asking to send something, I'm not a threat. I'm not asking to *talk* with someone. Just send them something. And I don't ask specifically for the sales manager, marketing manager, general manager, president, or CEO. Every company has a different decision-maker who buys what I sell. If the person I'm talking with doesn't know, he'll usually ask me one or two follow-up questions to determine who the contact is and then surrender the name.

f. When I have the name, I ask if it would be best to send the information by email or mail. If I'm lucky I'll get the email. If not, that's okay; I'll attach a note saying, "Bailey suggested I send this to your attention."

g. Once I get the information, I end the call with, "Great. I'll send it today and if you don't mind, I'll call back next week to make sure you've received it okay."

Can you see an important principle I've set into motion with this 10 second script? Commitment and consistency. Once the prospect stayed on the phone without hanging up, the technique began. He's committed to hear what I have to say.

If he gives me the name of the decision-maker, he's committed to the relationship. By volunteering the email or mailing address, the connection is strengthened. By the time I say, "...if you don't mind, I'll call back later…," he's going to remain consistent with his answers. He's gone too far to say no. Besides, he's thinking I'm the typical 95% salesperson: I either won't follow-up and send the information, or I won't call back. Guess what? I'm not. I'm a 5% salesperson. A 5%er does what 95% of the other salespeople don't do.

Your calls may have a different strategy than mine. Your strategy may be to close the deal on the first call. Maybe it's to get the appointment. Maybe it's to get information. Or give information. Many Internet companies today merely want to drive people to their websites. You decide.

But you've only got 20 seconds. Don't blow it.

21

End Run Around Gatekeepers

8 Options to Score

What about those pesky gatekeepers? Aren't they a nuisance? Let's do this, let's just beat them up, cheat, lie – anything to get around them to get to that Golden Decision-Maker waiting for us with pen in hand anxious to sign our contract and make us rich.

Gotta' Start Somewhere
This may not be the solution, but at least it's a beginning.

> *- C.J. Craig*
> *The West Wing*

A guy from Kansas City tried doing this to one of our gatekeepers when he called to register for our seminar. He was trying to cheat and cajole and get a free ticket by saying things that weren't true. He tried to intimidate her. He bad mouthed her. She held her ground. Finally, frustrated that he wasn't getting his way, he demanded to speak with the decision-maker (i.e. me). My gatekeeper said certainly. Let me see if he's in. She walked into my office and told me it was James. (Our company had a past history with him when he cheated us and our attendees at a seminar three years earlier. Guess he didn't think we'd remember him.)

I picked up the phone. "Hi James, what can I do for you?"

He was fuming. Wanted to come to our seminar again but the gatekeeper wouldn't give him a free ticket or cut him a deal. "You know," he said, "you ought to get rid of her. She's bad for your company."

I listened patiently as James vented. Finally the steam ran out. My turn.

"James, did you know that was my oldest daughter you were talking to?"

"Oh."

"James, she didn't know this, but I do. You tried this same call last week, saying almost the same things to another one of my gatekeepers. You probably didn't know the person you were trying to beat up with your tactics, but that gatekeeper was my wife."

"Oh."

You never know who the gatekeeper's married to or how they're related. Every gatekeeper is someone's son or daughter, wife or husband. Treat them with respect and dignity. They deserve it. They're loyal. They work hard. And they usually influence the decision-maker more than you know.

Knowing this, let's look at some legitimate ways, respectful ways to connect with the people we want to reach. Here are some ideas other attendees from across the country have shared with me that work. I've used them all, and they do as advertised. I've shown them to other salespeople to have them test the ideas. Worked for them too.

Paul Revere technique

A lady in Boston told me that she'll call to a company's rollover phone number around 5:15 p.m. No later than 5:30. The rollover phone number is the number in the next logical sequence behind the company's main number. Let's say the company's main number is 939-5300. Around 5:15, call 939-5301. If you call the main number after hours the phone empties into the company's voicemail. The next number in line is unconnected. It rings and rings and rings until someone answers it. What she and I found was that around 5:15 someone's still in the office waiting for their spouse to call with the grocery list. Their spouse has been given this "secret" number to reach them after hours.

I've done this successfully many times. Maybe the service manager picks up the line. Be upfront. Identify yourself. Tell her what you want.

"Hi. This is Jerry Hocutt with You've Got Contacts. I'd like to give your company two free sales tools to help increase your sales. I was calling to see…who could I send some information to at your company about this free service?"

"Oh," the manager replies, "that would be Betsy Frye. She's our president. Hey, she's standing here next to me. Wanna' talk with her?"

People after-hours aren't trained to be gatekeepers or screen calls. They'll be glad to give you a hand.

Second City technique

Talking with one of our attendees after our Chicago program, she told me she was in the bookkeeping department of her company. I was surprised.

"Why, this is a sales seminar. What brought you here?"

She laughed. "My boss sent me. He wanted me to spy on you and the salespeople and see what you talk about at a sales seminar."

My turn to laugh. "So what do you think of the salespeople you met here?"

"I was surprised. They're very nice. Professional. They really want to help the customer."

"In that case," I wanted to know, "do you have any helpful ideas for how to get around gatekeepers that you feel are acceptable and professional?"

"Sure," she said. "When you call and get the receptionist, immediately ask to speak with Accounts Receivable. Don't ask for Accounts Payable. They're not happy campers. We've been at the company long enough to know everyone there. If you're upfront with us, we can point you in the right direction."

Other variations of this: ask to speak to someone in sales – all salespeople take their calls; ask for someone in the service department; or the shipping department.

That's Life
Golf is a game of endless predicaments.
- Chi Chi Rodriguez

Brotherly Love technique

An attendee in Philadelphia told me that he'll call and when he gets the receptionist he asks for the service department. But the secret, he said, is to RAISE your voice just a little. Like something broke and you're upset.

"The receptionist is thinking, 'Uh-oh. Another problem. Hot potato. Don't have the time for this.' And then she connects me immediately with service. I'm upfront, tell them what I want and they'll always give me the name and extension I'm looking for."

Big Apple technique

A man who attended our New York seminar told me that after several calls of trying to reach his party, he'll call to an extension on either side of the one he's trying to reach.

"What do you mean?" I asked.

"Well, for example, I know the person I want to reach; but every time I call I'm dropped directly into his voicemail. After that happens four or five times I'll call the next extension up or down. Chances are, they're sitting next to each other. If my buyer, Ned, is at extension 235, I'll call to either extension 234 or 236. Nancy may pick up. 'Oh, Nancy? I'm sorry. I meant to call Ned at extension 235. Is he in by any chance?'"

"Sure. He's sitting here next to me. Wait a minute." Pause. "Hey! Ned. Line 2's for you."

Space Needle technique

This is one I stumbled on by myself and it works like a charm.

Selling Motorola 2-way radios, one of my vertical markets included hospitals in Seattle. Many departments could use the portable devices and often there was no central buyer. Sometimes it was purchasing. Sometimes facilities. Sometimes the individual departments had the authority.

When doing telephone cold calls to find the decision-maker I almost always got the hospital's voicemail directory. "If you know the extension of the person you want to reach, enter it now. If not, press #1 to hear a company directory."

Voicemail is today's ultimate gatekeeper.

Not knowing who or what department to ask for, I found the hospital's voicemail directory allowed employees to leave a short outgoing message. The voicemail directory had the first word. "Extension 45." Then the extension's owner came on. "Hi, this is Bill. I'll be in meetings all morning, but returning at 2 p.m. Leave your message."

I would listen to several outgoing messages like this and pick out three or four voices that sounded upbeat and positive. Once I had the names, I would then call directly to those extensions.

"Hi Bill, this is Jerry Hocutt and I'm sure you're not the person I should be speaking with at Children's Hospital about our Motorola 2-way radios. But do you have any idea who I should call?"

I would say this whether I was talking with the person live or if I was leaving a voicemail message. If I left a voicemail message with this request, I was surprised that they would do the research for me, find the name, and call me back. My return call rate was over 90%.

I picked up three of the largest hospitals in Seattle using this technique. Once the party I was talking with gave me the name, I would then call that extension and begin by saying, "Bill referred you to me as the person I should talk with about our radios." By saying I was referred, the decision-maker didn't know how well I knew the other party and always listened to what I had to say.

And if the first extension I called wasn't of any help or didn't want to talk with me, I'd call the next person on my list. It's not rocket science.

Chamber of Commerce technique

Not sure who makes the decisions for what you sell? The Internet and companies' websites make it easier – if you're upfront with them.

We wanted to find and then contact the decision-makers for our D-I-Y Sales & Marketing Email Postcards™ at several hundred companies throughout the U.S. Rather than taking the time and expense of making telephone cold calls, I decided to try another one of my experiments.

We'd find the names of different chambers of commerce throughout the country. Most chambers list the names of their members which includes their phone numbers, and email and website addresses.

If the member had an email address, we'd send a quick note like this: "I see that you're a member of the Austin Chamber of Commerce. I'd like to send some information to your company about our Viral Email Postcard Marketing™ program that's guaranteed to generate sales leads. Would you send me your mailing address? And whose attention I would send it to?" (Note: if they publish their email for public consumption, it's not spamming unless you're "harvesting" thousands of emails for the specific purpose of spamming. Just don't abuse the permission, keep your message on point, and never send attachments. For up-to-date information on spamming see www.ftc.gov).

Contact Us technique

If they didn't have an email address, we'd go to their Contact Us section on their website where they invited emails and send the same message. This technique got us the correct name 95% of the time.

There are three critical things about the emails for this and the Chamber of Commerce techniques. First, let them know you want to *send* information and not call. Sending isn't threatening; calling is.

Men Have Never Asked for Directions
I have never been lost, but I will admit to being confused for several weeks.

- Daniel Boone

Second, put the questions in the correct sequence. Ask for their address first (even if it's plastered all over their website). By asking for something they know the answer to (an easy, no-brainer question) you start getting answers. You start commitment and consistency using email. Then ask whose attention you'd send the information to. The name almost always pops out. But timing of the questions is critical. If you ask for the name before the address, your responses will be significantly lower.

Third, use the words *will* or *would* when you request the address. "*Would* you send me your mailing address?" Don't use the words *can* or *could*. This is based upon Allan and Barbara Pease's research (*Why Men Don't Listen and Women Can't Read Maps*). They found that men interpret words literally. Women don't. Thus, the words *will* or *would* won't work on women. Men interpret *can* or *could* as, "Do you have the *ability*?" Men think, "Sure. Of course I *could*. But I'm *not*."

But *will* or *would*, the Pease's found, asks for a *commitment*. Either you will or you won't. Once they make a commitment (there's that darn commitment and consistency thing again), they'll follow-up with their promise. They use the example of when a man asks a woman to marry him. He doesn't ask, "*Can* you marry me?" but "*Will* you marry me?"

The reason you use *will* or *would* in your email is because you don't know who's reading it – male or female. You might as well stack the odds in your favor.

Once I had the name, I would then send the information saying who referred me and that I would be calling soon to follow-up. The email got my foot in the door; the follow-up blew the door down.

Even though we worked with an excellent list broker for over a decade, we still found this to be the most accurate and least expensive technique for getting the right names; and it's excellent to use if you're looking for a small list of about 200-500 names at a time.

The GM technique

The GM technique is used to drive people to our website. It works extremely well by using their voicemail as my tool. You know what a cold calling blitz is: all the salespeople concentrate on one salesperson's territory and flood it with cold calls to try and find business.

The GM technique is a variation of this. It's what I call a marketing blitz. The goal is to make the maximum number of contacts in the shortest possible time. It's not to overwhelm those who resist, but to create awareness.

The concept is that your website or blog becomes your E-brochure. Because you're trying to drive as many people to your site as possible, this is one of the few times you'll give up the initiative and let them connect with you if they're interested.

We do a lot of business with hotel sales staffs. I wanted to get my message to the general managers of the hotels. The GM's have the leverage to pass the information to their sales staff, and in effect, it becomes a top-down referral. This technique is so absurdly simple that I'm embarrassed to share it with others.

Call the hotel. If you get the switchboard or front desk, ask for the general manager's voicemail. You don't need to identify yourself or your company. You don't need to say what the call is about.

"Good morning, Marriott Cambridge," the operator answers.

"Will you give me the general manager's voicemail, please?"

Click, whirr, I get his voicemail. Keep in mind that I don't even know the name of the general manager. And because I asked for the general manager's voicemail and not to speak to the manager personally, the operator must think I'm either a guest or I know the general manager well enough to leave a voicemail message. I'm no threat to the gatekeeper or the general manager since I'm going to voicemail jail anyway.

Guess how the general manager starts his outgoing message? With his name. And just like that, I have his name if I ever want to call back to follow-up (remember I keep records on all my contacts).

I leave my quick 20-30 second voicemail promoting our website. I also mention that if he or his sales manager visits the site they can get one of our free ebooks. I use the free ebooks to measure the effectiveness of the GM technique. If I leave 100 messages a day, and see 50-60 of those ebooks are downloaded, I know the program is working.

This is an extremely easy-to-use technique, is non-threatening if you're afraid of cold calling, and gets immediate results.

Oh yeah, the results. When I call asking for the general manager's voicemail, 99% of the time I get it. The 1% of the time I don't? I get to speak directly with the GM. I found that the larger the organization you call, the more likely that GM is to pick up his or her own phone. The smaller Marriott properties almost always go to voicemail. But with the larger Marriott properties in Boston, New York, Philadelphia, Miami, Dallas, and Atlanta the GM's answer their own phones. They're not afraid to talk with anyone.

There you have eight tried and proven techniques to deal better with the gatekeepers, get the information you want, and help the people who want your help. An end run with eight options. Touchdown!

22

The Eliminator

Voicemail: Love It or Leave It?

You're cold calling. You're sent to the decision-maker's voicemail.

"Leave your message at the tone…be-e-e-e-p."

Do you? Or don't you?

It depends. What's your strategy? Can you Jujitsu their voice-mail and turn it to your advantage?

Voicemail is like fire: if you use it correctly it can warm you and feed you. Use it the wrong way and you'll burn down the house.

One mistake salespeople make is trying to sell their service or product with their voicemail message. Mission impossible. Don't try it.

That's Crazy
Ordinarily he was insane, but he had lucid moments when he was merely stupid.
- Heinrich Heine

I got a lengthy voicemail from a printer. It was a cold call from a complete stranger. I've never met or talked with her. Said she knew our company printed a lot of brochures. She went on to tell me how much better their company was than my current vendor, gave me some ballpark figures for costs, and reasons I should do business with her.

"I'd like for you to come by and tour our new facility. We're really proud of it. But the real reason I'd like you to stop by," she said, "is to meet and talk with my managers. This would make me look good and be a big coup for me if I could get the appointment."

Couple of problems with this message. First, we have no relationship and she's trying to convince me to do business with her on a voicemail message. Second, I could care less about touring her new facility. I'm sure it's nice and they're proud of it, but I travel constantly and when I get back into town, I don't have the time to look at equipment that has no interest for me. All I want to know is can you get the job done right or not?

Finally, the "real reason" for me to take a couple of hours out of my day and stop by was to make her look good to her managers. I may be old fashioned, but isn't the salesperson supposed to make the customer look good? I didn't know the customer had to make the salesperson look good.

Use voicemail to sell one of three things:

1. Sell the prospect to take your call when you call again.
2. Sell the prospect to return your call.
3. Or sell the appointment.

Don't use it to sell your service or product.

Who are you? Who? Who?

What if the CEO's assistant says, "She's in a meeting, would you like her voicemail?" Would you dare go there?

Nod your head. On the first cold call, I usually won't leave a message, but I do want to listen to the CEO's outgoing message. Like CSI's Gil Grissom, I'm looking for clues.

How does she pronounce her name? Does she talk fast? Slow? Leave a lot of details? Is she abrupt? Does she use the personal pronouns "I" and "me" multiple times? Maybe her message says what time she'll be returning. If she's out of town, when I call back I'll ask, "How was your trip?"

How did you know? Are you a psychic?

No one can sell like you

In interviews with gatekeepers I asked, "What clues are you listening for from salespeople who cold call?"

"The first thing," they told me, "is to see if the salesperson will agree to go to the boss's voicemail."

Why?

The gatekeepers said if they go to the voicemail it means the salesperson must know the boss and is comfortable in leaving a message. But if they say, "No, I'll call back," the clue is they don't know the boss, this is a cold call, and they'll make an impression of that salesperson's voice. If the salesperson calls again, they'll double their efforts to make sure he never gets put through.

Another advantage of leaving a quick voicemail message is that you can leave accurate information with enthusiasm. If a gatekeeper asks if I'd like to leave a message with him or go to the boss's voicemail, I always ask for voicemail.

A left message with a gatekeeper might be reported like this. "Some salesman – uh – don't remember his name – called and wanted to ask you about...uh...something to do with...uh...our copiers. No, wait, something about our telephones? No, that was some other guy. Heck, I don't remember. Never mind. He'll probably call back."

Leaving voicemail messages creates frequency of contact. Frequency of contact is a marketing strategy. We mentioned earlier that people have to see you, see your name, or hear your name six times before they'll trust you enough to buy from you. Voicemail can count for all six contacts.

911, Do You Have an Emergency?
When tempted to "fight fire with fire," remember that the fire department usually uses water.
- Unknown

Add value to your messages

When you leave messages, don't get on the person's case. "Will you please call me back?" "This is my third call. I'd really like to talk with you. Please call me back."

Be different. When calling, leave a new marketing or sales idea they can use or share with their staff. I keep a list of ideas I've found in magazines, on the Internet, in books, or from the newspaper by my phone. If I get their voicemail, I'll say something like, "Sorry I missed you. I'll try to reach you in a couple of days. Oh, just read an article in *Selling Power*. Said that a 2% customer retention rate is equivalent to cutting your sales costs by 10%.

Thought you'd want to pass that on to your sales managers at your next meeting. Call you later."

By saying I'll "call you later" I'm able to keep the initiative and call back when I'm ready. I don't want to put the ball in his court and depend upon him to take the initiative to call me back.

Why do I want to listen to the person's outgoing message? Personalities are revealed in the words, sentences, and tones of voice they use. Does she sound up? Down? Monotone? Does she use short words and short sentences? Long words and long sentences? Does she leave detailed information? Is she emotional? Important clues that will help me to change and adapt to her listening and thinking style when we do make contact. (How to interpret these in later chapters.)

Kelly in Chicago shared this next idea. She attended our seminar and told me why she was so successful with voicemail. She led her company in getting the most calls taken and returned.

Kelly said that every morning she goes to HistoryChannel.com to find what events occurred on this date in history. If she gets voicemail when cold calling she leaves a quick message and then adds, "You know on this date in history...."

She also puts another event on her outgoing message each day. When she picks up her messages later she hears "click" "click" "click". Kelly said people are calling in to her voicemail just to hear the event of the day and then hang-up.

Today, I use a variation of this. I have my own sales and marketing blog I update daily. If I get someone's voicemail I'll tell them to, "Check out today's blog and learn the types of handshakes decision-makers use." With page counters on the blog, I can judge the effectiveness of my cold calls by seeing how many readers go to the handshake page.

What decision-makers look for

In interviews with decision-makers, I asked them, "What do you look for in a good voicemail message? What would encourage you to call the salesperson back?"

First: tell them who you are. "Don't play games with me. Don't try to trick me. If you have an unusual name, spell it." If you can give them a hook to hang it on, even better. "This is Jerry Hocutt. H-o-c-u-t-t. It's like a half-cut, but a ho-cutt." People laugh but they remember it. "Oh, *Half*cutt. Yeah, I remember you."

Second: tell them what company you're with. It's a point of reference.

Third: tell them what you want. "I'd like to give your company two free sales tools to help increase your sales."

Leave Your Problem at the Tone
Problems are messages.
- Shakti Gawain

The sales manager of a Fortune 500 company in Chicago came to the stage after one of our seminars. He was a little upset. "I wish you wouldn't have told our salespeople to do those first three things when leaving messages. We tell them to do exactly the opposite."

Oh?

"We tell them: don't identify yourself. Don't tell them the name of the company. And don't tell them what you want. Play mind games with them."

O-o-o-kay. "So…how are your sales going?"

"They *stink*! That's why we came here today."

Hmm. Deceit. Mind games. Gee, I wonder why.

Some people say they'll try to trick a prospect into returning their call. "We found out something important about your company that your competitor…." And then they hang-up like they've been disconnected. They ask me what I think about this ploy.

I wouldn't do it. That's not me. Besides, what if you do trick them into calling you back? They see the ruse. What's happened to your credibility? Remember – 71% of the purchasing decision is based upon trust. I get better results by being upfront. Besides, I can take rejection. He-y-y-y!

As I told the Chicago sales manager, "Look, if what you're doing works for you now, continue doing it regardless of what I say. However, if what you're doing isn't working, you may want to consider tweaking it and making some changes. If your voicemail strategies aren't working, deep-six them and try something else."

Finally, the fourth thing decision-makers look for, which I was not aware of until we did the survey, was, "Tell me what you want *me* to do. Are you calling me back? Are you sending me information? Am I supposed to call you back? What do you want man? I'm too busy to read your mind."

This supports earlier research that the Gallup Organization conducted with San Jose State University. They found that managers, on average, send and receive over 178 messages per day. And this isn't even counting email! Employees walk in. Calls from the field. Other managers have input, want ideas. Clients call. Service people need help. Bookkeeping wants to know when to invoice. Accounts receivable wants to know where the money is. They have twenty conversations at Rotary before lunch is served.

You're not going to hurt their feelings by being direct. And don't let them hurt yours when they are, too. That's just the way they operate.

Orange County voicemail

When we were doing our first seminar in Orange County, we cold called newspapers in the area to see if they'd do trade-outs with us. If they'd give us free advertising, we'd give them free seats to the seminar for their salespeople.

Zeus!
You are not in charge of the universe; you are in charge of yourself.
- A. Bennett

Before the call, we sent a one-page proposal to the publishers outlining the desired trade-out. When I called to follow-up, I was sometimes sent to the publisher's voicemail. Because I was making hundreds of cold calls, I wasn't going to call back. Besides, I wanted to try what our interviews uncovered: be direct and tell them what I wanted them to do.

My message ended with this statement: "I won't be calling you back. (I wanted them to know this was the first and last call.) But if you would like to participate in this program, you must return my call by February 15."

Results? I left ten voicemail messages with ten publishers. Seven of the ten called me back personally. Three of those seven did business with us on the spot. We got hundreds of thousands of free advertising impressions with a very effective voicemail. I would have never known this would work if the decision-makers hadn't shared their thoughts with me.

But we had some leverage. Our seminar was mid-March. We'd only be in Orange County once that year. Deadlines for action help. Ask any negotiator. The newspapers had to act by mid-February. After that, the game's over. If you can have a deadline before the event expires, or the sale ends, you can leave a forceful message like we did.

You can make it, girl

If you don't, try this technique one of our attendees in Minneapolis shared with the group. After several calls to the prospect, and upon getting no response, she'll leave this message: "I've left several voicemail messages with you, but guess you're not in the market at this time. I don't want to wear out my welcome, so I won't be calling back for three or four months. But – if you're interested – please let me know."

I asked her, "What's your call return rate?"

Her eyes widened, eyebrows arched, "They went up over 30%!" But she didn't know why that message worked so well. Neither did I.

Getting back to Seattle, I experimented with her message. I got about the same increase of returned calls. I gave the idea to several companies and asked them to have their salespeople try the technique. Worked for them as well.

I think what happened is the lady in Minneapolis put it all on the line. She didn't come across as desperate. She said that many of those who did call back immediately started the conversation, "I'm sorry. I meant to call you back, but we're so busy working on our budgets. I really am interested. Please don't give up on me. Why don't you call me in three weeks?"

But for those who never called back, she kept her foot in the door and she kept the initiative. After three months she'd call them again. "Hi, this is Pam. I left you a message three months ago saying I'd call you back this week. I wanted to keep my promise and follow-up. Are you still in the market for our services?"

Voicemail. Love it. Leave it. But don't ignore it.

23

Voicemail Jail Break

How to Create Your Voicemail Script

The Wizard of Ads: Turning Words into Magic and Dreamers into Millionaires, by Roy H. Williams, is an excellent source for how to create more effective letters, proposals, and voicemail messages. The chapter "Look for the Loophole!" shows you how to get rid of the blah words that numb people's minds.

The concept is to first create your voicemail message and then after each statement put in parenthesis what you think the recipient is really thinking. Once you get a better understanding, you can go back and create a more effective script.

How to Understand Teenagers
If you want to truly understand something, try to change it.

- Kurt Lewin

For example, we've done work with hundreds of chambers of commerce across the U.S. Like any other business, some are at the top of their game and some don't even know they're in the game. One of our chamber attendees on the East coast asked me why so few of their sales staff ever got their voicemail messages returned. He gave me a sample of their script; the purpose of their calls was to increase membership in the chamber.

I told him that one reason people may not return his calls is because they can see through him. He never gave prospects specific information as to how he could benefit them. Prospects know that if anyone benefits in the chamber/member relationship, the chamber is looking out for #1.

To get better results, I told him, you have to get people to change what they're thinking about you. Before leaving a message, try to understand what's going through their minds. Write out your script and after each statement you make, imagine what the prospects are thinking. Then you'll see what you need to change.

Here's an actual call I received from a local chamber in the Seattle area.

"Hi, this is Fred..." (I'm not expecting a call from a Fred) "...with the Humongous Chamber of Commerce." (Aarrgh! Chambers are a waste.) "I'd like for you to call me back." (Fat chance.)

"I think we could have a great partnership and work well together." (Yeah, right. All you want is my membership fee.) "Why don't you call me back and we can discuss all the benefits of..." (Click.)

If you want to change what your prospect is thinking, change what you're saying.

"Hi Jerry." (Got my attention. He must know me.) "I just visited your website…" (I'm impressed you took the time to find it) "…and I see that your company helps small businesses find customers for their business." (You've done your homework.)

"I'm Fred with the Humongous Chamber of Commerce…" (uh-oh, knew there was a catch) "…and I have three members who might be interested in your help." (Hmm. He's willing to give me referrals?) "If you'd like to give me a call, I can give you more information on them." (It's a ruse. You're just trying to sell me a membership.) "And no, I won't try to sell you a membership unless you're interested in learning more about us." (Maybe he knows what he's doing. Might be worth the call.)

Do people see through you? If so, do your homework. Be specific. Put them first. Get your message out, get it heard, and get the call back.

24

Getting Rid of the Blahs

If You're Going to Send a Letter Before You Call

Sometimes you may want to send a letter or email before you make your cold call; just as we sent the one page proposal to the newspaper publishers for our Orange County seminar. The purpose of the letter was to improve our odds that our phone calls would be taken when we followed up. It also gave us the ability to fully explain our proposition without wasting valuable telephone time.

Reading Lips
If you want to get rich from writing, write the sort of thing that's read by persons who move their lips when reading.

- Don Marquis

There are two superb books on writing business letters. Padraic Spence, *Write Smart...and Get Decisions: The Complete Guide to*

Business Writing, refers to his DOC (Decision-Oriented Correspondence) which can be anything from writing a business memo, a trip report, a letter, or an email. His objective is to be short, get to the point, and get a decision.

The second great book is Roy Williams' *The Wizard of Ads*. Using Williams' concept of closing the loopholes and getting rid of blah words that put customers in a daze, let's look at a letter you might write to a prospect. After each statement, to close the loopholes, put in parenthesis what you think the prospect is thinking.

> Dear Mr. Jackson,
> *(What do you want? You're bothering me.)*
> I'm sure you have a lot of printing needs…
> *(We've got a printer. Leave me alone.)*
> …and because of our new MegaDeluxe printer…
> *(Wonder what's for dinner tonight?)*
> …we can beat any competitor's prices in town.
> *(Did I trim my toenails last night?)*
> Just call us for a bid on your next….
> *(Blah-blah-blah-blah. Is it getting foggy in
> here? I think I just saw my life flash in front of
> my eyes.)*

Sound like hundreds of letters you forget each year? Using the technique of closing the loopholes, you cannot only make your letter rise to the top of the pile, but the technique gets you to speak in a more personal tone and even add some humor to get your point across.

For example, here's a marketing letter I've created using this technique. After each statement, supply your own thoughts in parenthesis. And then decide which of the two letters are more likely to leave an impression in a prospect's mind.

This letter is sent to sales managers to drive them to our website. The prospect's name, address, and salutation have been eliminated so I can get to the point quickly.

> *This will be quick so I don't have time for a salutation. Besides, you know your name and my wife won't let me call anyone Dear but her.*
>
> *Guess your salespeople are busy knockin' down the doors and beating the bushes to find new customers. I'm sure your desk is full of their monthly sales reports so you can see the progress they're making. If a salesperson leaves, I imagine you know who their accounts' contacts are so they won't do a disappearing act with them.*
>
> *If you need help keeping the boss off your back, we can help your salespeople connect to sell. They'll turn prospects into customers and increase referrals, cross-selling, and customer retention.*
>
> *You can monitor each salesperson's activities so you'll be sure they're doing what they're supposed to be doing. They'll never consider taking a lunch break again.*
>
> *And kiss your non-compete contract clauses goodbye. Your salespeople can't hide their contact information on their accounts any longer. The minute the salesperson leaves in a huffy-fit, you can contact their orphaned accounts quicker than you can click your email Send.*

This will keep the boss off your back. Guess I said that already. Geez, he must be a tough cookie. Hate to be in your shoes.

Anyway, if you're looking for help, meet me at YouveGotContacts.com before it's too late.

Gotta' go. Time's up. Call me. Write to me. I'll hold my breath.

Jerry Hocutt

P.S. By the way, get out your checkbook. This will cost you an arm and a leg. Keeping the boss off your back isn't cheap.

I don't tell them I'm calling to follow-up. But when I do, I tell them I'm the guy who sent the letter to get the boss off their back. They laugh and remember.

If you think this letter will generate some negative fallout from a few recipients, you're right. We want it to. Williams points out that if you soften the words, letters, or ads so that it offends no one, says nothing, and sounds like every other letter, you'll keep getting zero results.

Got It
Communication is the art of being understood.
- Peter Ustinov

We learned how powerful words can be in 1992 when we named our national seminars Cold Calling for Cowards®. People sit up and notice; most like the name and can identify with it while others may become angry and call to tell us so. (Of course, they are always afraid to tell us their name and hang-up quickly.) But we get the reaction we want. And the success!

If you want to change what people are doing, you've got to change what they're thinking. To change what they're thinking, you've got to change what you're saying.

25

The Best Question to Ask on a First Sales Call

Revealing Personalities

 "Is now a good time?"

"Do you have a minute?"

Ask either question and you'll get a wealth of information. But if you ask, "Hey, how are you today?" that ringing sound you hear in your ear is called a dial tone.

"How are you today?" is a sign you don't know what else to say or why you're even saying it. People know you don't care. They know you're not listening. It's your attempt at small talk and 65% of the people you call on don't have time for it.

Let's Get Ready to Rum-m-m-mble!
When women kiss, it always reminds me of prize fighters shaking hands.

- H.L. Mencken

When you ask, "Is now a good time?" people will respond in one of four ways.

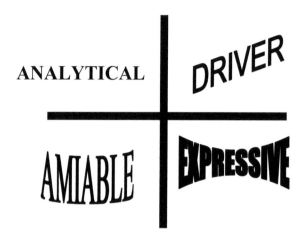

The **Driver's** response: "What do you want? What's this about?" They're blunt. Get to the point. Drivers like to do the talking. Be careful not to interrupt them. And don't ask a lot of questions. They don't like the tables turned on them. They account for 15% of the people you call on.

The **Analytical**: "No. I'm on my way to a meeting. Call me back next week." You call next week. "Is now a good time?" His response is, "Sorry on my way to lunch. Call me Friday afternoon." You call Friday afternoon and like Elvis, he's left the building. It's the Analytical's response that scares people from asking "Is now a good time?" They think everyone responds this way. But it's only the Analyticals. They're looking for excuses not to talk with you. Analyticals make up 35% of the people you speak with.

The **Amiable**: "Oh, hi. You bet. Let's talk." They're comfortable in talking with anyone. They're the 35% who are comfortable with small talk.

The **Expressive**: "Sure. Fine. Go ahead." Expressives sound like Drivers. Both use short words and short sentences. The big difference is that Expressives have a friendlier tone in their voice. Only 15% of the people you speak with fall into this category.

Analyticals and Amiables use longer words and longer sentences. That's why I like to listen to people's outgoing voicemail messages. To see if they use short words and short sentences (Drivers and Expressives) or long words and long sentences (Analyticals and Amiables). Now when I talk with them, I'll know how to adjust my conversation.

Also, by knowing their personalities it tells me how long this selling cycle will be.

Drivers can make a decision in 1-2 calls. That means he or she can make a decision on this very first call. So be prepared. And stay away from small talk. Drivers hate it.

Expressives can make a decision in 2-3 calls. Center your call around them. They love to talk about themselves and will carry most of the conversation. Like Drivers, you need to be direct in dealing with them, but appeal more to their emotions.

Amiables can make a decision in 4-5 calls. The problem is, they're dependent upon other people helping them make the decision. Find out who they're going to for advice and get them involved in the process. Like Analyticals, they're indirect in dealing with you.

Analyticals can make a decision in 5-7 calls. Analyticals, like Drivers, are often top-level decision-makers and are found in upper-management. Never back them into a corner for a decision. They'll make a decision once they get all the facts. And make sure you have them, because if you don't, they'll hold it against you.

They have the memory of an elephant, so don't think you can come back and try another day if you haven't been upfront.

When you're calling on customers for the first time, every word counts. Don't waste them or the opportunity.

What's the magic number?

When do you give up calling? Consider this:

>44% of salespeople give up after the first call.
>22% stop after the second.
>14% after the third.
>12% stop after the fourth call.

That means that 92% of all salespeople stop calling after four calls.

Now consider the information staring you in the face. 70% of the people you call on (Amiables and Analyticals) won't even make a decision until you get beyond that fourth call. If there's a magic number, it's five.

But if your very first call goes like this, "Jerry, if you *ever* try to call me again, I'm calling my attorney and the state police!" you're done here. You've reached a Driver. He made a decision. Live with it.

But if they keep putting you off, you're probably dealing with the Analytical or Amiable.

Does that mean that after five calls you give up and never call again? No. It means it's time for a cooling off period. If I've identified they're doing business with my competitor, I never give up. I stay connected because I know these are Level 2 prospects and I know things will change. I keep in touch because I want to position myself to be #2 on their list until they call me, making me #1.

In the story about Socrates I said that 70% of prospects try to avoid problems. The Amiables and Analyticals. It's only the Drivers and Expressives who are looking for opportunities and benefits.

If you know what you're looking for, you'll know what to ask. Now you know[2].

P.S. There are exceptions to every rule. If you sell health care products or services, or if you solicit for charities related to health care, the best question to ask would be, "How are you today?" Whether they say yes or no, your questioning can lead them into how to feel better or help others to feel better.

26

It Seemed Simple at the Time

The One Who Makes the Fewest Mistakes Wins

Here's a simple exercise you've seen before. If you want to win a free lunch from your co-workers, make a copy of this page and have them do the exercise as well.

Count the number of "F's" in this sentence.

> **FINISHED FILES ARE THE RE-SULT OF YEARS OF SCIENTIF-IC STUDY COMBINED WITH THE EXPERIENCE OF MANY YEARS.**

How many did you count? Three, right? Four? Five? Six?

There are six. The majority of people will catch the three obvious ones: FINISHED; FILES; SCIENTIFIC. Some will catch four. A few more will see five. But only 10% of people will find all six.

Still can't see them? Look at the word "OF". It's in the sentence three times.

"Oh, yeah," you moan, "now I see them."

Why didn't you see them the first time? Psychologists say it's because we pronounce the word *of* as *uv*, not *of*, and the mind simply overlooks it.

If you had a strategy, you could have found all three. For example, in the Air Force we learned how to read sentences backwards. If you read this in reverse you should catch all six. When you read it backwards the sentence makes no sense and forces your brain to pay extra attention to each word.

Another strategy? Turn the page upside down. It turns the left brain (logical, sequential, word side) off and activates the right (creative) side of the brain. Because the mind has to work harder and pay closer attention, you'll be able to see all the F's. One of my top ten favorite books is *Drawing on the Right Side of the Brain* by Betty Edwards. Edwards teaches you to turn off the left brain and turn on the right brain by having you draw pictures upside down. Your fourth drawing in the book will be your Picasso and it'll blow you away how easily you can draw it and how great it looks.

Here's an easier strategy. I gave you the hard copy. I didn't put a time limit on it. All you had to do was get a pen, look at every single letter, and circle each F.

But you're thinking, "This is so easy any dodo can do this with his eyes closed."

This is one of the problems we have in turning cold calls into appointments and appointments into sales. The answers we're looking for are staring us in the face, but because we have no strategies we overlook the obvious answers.

Salespeople fail to grasp the importance of appointments. Appointments are like job interviews. The prospect can hire you or she can fire you. You can be invited back for the next interview, or never have your calls taken or returned. People aren't looking for reasons to do business with you. *They're looking for reasons to eliminate you.* Go ahead. Show up late. Don't send the information you promised. Be hard to find. Don't keep in touch and take my business for granted.

Comedy act

To turn cold calls into appointments, you'll need to master three skills: (a) keep your foot out of your mouth; (b) create a good first impression; and (c) think on your feet faster.

Make the Best of It
Golf is not a game of perfect.
> *- Tom Kite*

Sounds simple. It's not.

Jerry Seinfeld had a good routine about voicemail. He said, "Voicemail. Don't you get it? You don't need to say 'leave your message at the BEEP'. They know there's going to be a BEEP. They know to leave a message. And what's this thing about telling them to leave their name and phone number? You don't need to tell them. People get it."

Not so fast Mr. Seinfeld. Leaving town to do some seminars, I left on my outgoing message, "Please leave your name, number, and a brief message no longer than one minute at the tone."

Listening to my messages that night, one caller left a *five* minute message. Five minutes! I never go back and listen to a message that long; but he did something unusual. I thought maybe I missed it. I played the message again. Nope. I was right. He left a five minute message but he never left his phone number! I couldn't believe it. He's probably wondering to this day why I never called him back.

Stupid is as stupid does

Don't do stupid things. A local paper had a story about some of the stupid things people do on job interviews. Executives responsible for hiring at 200 of the nation's largest companies said applicants are saying goodbye within minutes of their first hello to the interviewer. They were asked, "What is the most unusual or humorous incident you recall during an interview for an entry-level position?"

Response: "The reason the candidate was taking so long to respond to a question became apparent when he began to snore."

Response: "Why did he go to college? His ill-conceived answer: 'To party and socialize.'"

Response: "Said she had graduated cum laude but had no idea what cum laude meant. However, she said she was proud of her grade point average. It was 2.1."

Response: "She actually showed up for an interview during the summer wearing a bathing suit. Said she didn't think I'd mind."

Response: "I had asked the candidate to bring a résumé and a couple of references. He arrived with the résumé – and two people."

The survey also uncovered some do's and don'ts for the aspiring employee. "Don't save your best for last; most interviewers make up their minds *within 15 minutes*. Most important, pay attention. Listen to the questions and give complete answers."

In other words, keep your foot out of your mouth, create a good first impression, and think on your feet. Don't do stupid things.

Hook, line, and stinker

More than once I've received cold calls like this.

"Hi Mr. Hocutt. I'm Jim with the (pick one: Mighty Fine Printing Consortium, No Body Beats Us Marketing Agency, or Best Damn List Broker Ever). How are you today?"

Nothing.

Awkward silence for Jim. Amusement for me.

"Anyway, I see that you do national sales seminars, is that right?"

Okay, I'll concede him a "Right" here.

"Great. You know," Jim says because he's really excited I've taken the bait, "that if you do business with us we can TRIPLE your sales and get more butts in those seats than ever before."

Now keep in mind that I've never heard of Jim or his company. Jim has never been to one of our seminars so he doesn't know how many people attend. Yet he can triple our sales. Jim has no idea how many brochures we send out, what our costs are, and what our percentage of sales to mailings ratio is. Yet, he can TRIPLE our sales.

Time for me to fake my excitement to match Jim's.

"Hey Jim, that's FANTASTIC! TRIPLE OUR SALES! MAN THAT'S AMAZING! YOU'VE REALLY GOT ME EXCITED NOW! I CAN'T BELIEVE IT. WHERE HAVE YOU BEEN ALL MY LIFE? THIS – IS – EXCITING!"

By now I'm sure that Jim is beside himself in excitement. Heck, he may have even wet his pants.

"Oh, Jim," I calm myself down now, "could you do me a favor?"

"YOU BET MR. HOCUTT! I'M REALLY EXCITED TO DO IT! JUST NAME IT!"

"Super. Jim, here's my fax number. If you'll just fax over to me your guarantee that you'll TRIPLE my sales by doing business with you – you know, give me something in writing – then once I get it, I'll give you a call back and we'll set an appointment to get started right away."

I've had about a half-dozen calls like Jim's. Never heard back from any of them.

Harvey Penick, the great golfing instructor, said it is the golfer *who makes the fewest mistakes who wins*. The same applies to sales. The salesperson who makes the fewest mistakes, the one who keeps his foot out of his mouth, is the one who gets the appointment.

Oh, Knock It Off
Never miss a good chance to shut up.
                              - Will Rogers

27

Only the Persuaded Can Persuade

What *Are* You Thinking?

Four things can stop us from turning our cold calls into appointments: our lack of confidence, not doing our homework, not studying the psychology of selling, and our beliefs.

One of my biggest sales discoveries came to me when driving to work one cold January day. Earlier in October, I had started work with the Fortune 1000 McCaw Communications. In November, I sold more than any rookie in the company's history. (Don't get excited. It wasn't that much. Overall, the company's yearly sales had been in the toilet.) In December, I barely made a blip on the sales board. Sales were miserable for all of us.

Things were so bad that our sales manager, Paul, was conducting two sales meetings a week trying to get us motivated, trying to find out what our problem was. Not one of our salespeople was meeting quota. No one was winning the sales contests; SPIFF's remained unclaimed. (You had to meet quota to even qualify for the monthly sales contests.) Everyone's job was in jeopardy. Sales-people were being fired or leaving faster than the ferries could leave Coleman dock.

A question that leads to discovery

At the end of December, after our last sales meeting, and before we'd break for the New Year, Paul pulled me aside.

"Jerry, why can't we meet quota? Why can't you meet quota? What's the problem?"

I didn't know what to say. I shrugged my shoulders. "Paul, don't you think if I knew, I'd be doing it myself?"

Better Get Your Rabies Shots
I bought a dog the other day...I named him Stay.
It's fun to call him..."Come here, Stay! Come
here, Stay!" He went insane.

- Steven Wright

I didn't tell Paul, but in December I had decided that if I didn't turn my sales around I was leaving at the end of January. I couldn't afford to keep the job, and they couldn't afford to keep me on.

Back to the first week of January. As I'm driving down Maple Valley hill, a picture flashed through my mind. The instant I saw it, I knew what my problem was.

I worked through the solution before reaching the office. That very day my sales turned. I won the first of many sales contests I'd claim over the next four years.

Our branch manager was watching closely. After the sales

meeting, after being presented my SPIFF, she called me into her office.

"Jerry," Connie began, "I noticed that your sales turned on (and she named the exact date). Do you mind telling me how you did it? I'd like to share it with the other salespeople because we really need help."

I told her I didn't want to tell her now. Let me try for two more months to see if it's the answer I'm looking for. If it was, I'd tell her. But if she wanted to find any volunteers who wanted to experiment with me, I'd show them what I was doing but not explain why or how it was working.

She jumped at the chance and went onto the sales floor and got some of my friends to volunteer. I met with each salesperson individually and showed them what to do, but told them not to ask me why or how it worked. They agreed.

For the next two months we all exceeded our goals for the first time. After the experiment was complete, I explained to our branch manager what I did and why I thought it worked. Connie asked me to mentor any other salesperson who would be interested in my discovery, which I did as long as I remained at McCaw.

A Kodak nanosecond

What was the picture that shot through my mind that January morning? What was it that turned things around for me? It was the flashback of our last sales meeting in December. The fleeting picture was that of all our salespeople sitting around the conference table with their heads down. Depressed. Defeated. Dejected. We didn't believe in what we were doing. And that was the problem. We didn't *believe*.

But, I asked myself, *what* didn't I believe?

I didn't believe in our *product* – the hardware. At the time we were selling Motorola pagers. But, I correctly reasoned, Motorola makes the best pager on the market. They're Six Sigma for goodness sake. No one made a better product. Now I believe in our product.

I didn't believe in the *need* for pagers. Probably smoke and mirrors. Until the mid-80's the biggest users of pagers were in the fields of medicine and construction. Few others used them. But, I thought, pagers save lives. Doctors and nurses have been reached in time to render aid. Pagers also save time. Trips across the floating bridges can be saved if customers can reach me to cancel or reschedule appointments. I can save my customers time the same way. I can be found quickly by customers who are ready to buy now. My customers can be found. Okay, I believe in the need for our product.

I don't believe in our *company*? It is the largest company I've worked for. Lots of bureaucracy. I had interviewed with some of our competitors, but chose McCaw. If our company was good enough for me, it should be good enough for my customers. And if it wasn't, I promised I would always tell our customers to do business with someone else. I do believe in our company.

What about our *management*? I trusted them. They sold me. And knowing what I did about our competitors, we had the best. Yeah, I believe in management.

See the Difference?
Price is what you pay. Value is what you get.

> *- Warren Buffett*

What about our *prices*? We were more expensive than our competitors. Our competitors had the same Motorola products. What made us different? Because our company had invested huge sums of capital to acquire more paging frequencies and transmitters to reach our customers more quickly wherever they were, and because they had put together the best sales, service, and management teams, we had the best *value* for the dollar. Shopping customers may equate price with identical hardware, but it was my job to educate them on the value. Price was no longer an issue. I believed in our *value*.

(Note: some people ask if I became McCaw's #1 salesman in the nation and salesman of the year because I "gave away" the business. Because of my strong beliefs about value v. price, our president congratulated me on leading the nation every year in *profits per pager* and *profits per account*.)

One belief bothered me and it took me several days to work it out. "Do I believe I can make the *money* I want? Would I run out of prospects, thus out of sales?" This is when I developed my Cake Recipe Theory mentioned previously. So, yes, I believed I could make the money I wanted.

BELIEFS

You...

-Have Best Product/Service
-Work For Best Company
-Have Best Value
-Are Best Salesperson

...For This Customer ...
At This Time

If you believe it, they'll know it

Beliefs. Before you pick up that telephone, you better believe that you have the best product or service for this customer at this time. You better believe that you work for the best company for this customer at this time. That you have the best value – not the best price – for this customer at this time. And you better believe that you're the best salesperson for this customer at this time.

If you don't truly believe this, guess where it shows up? In your voice. In less than two seconds. People's instincts tell them if you believe.

Notice I put a qualifier on the beliefs. "For this customer at this time".

There is no perfect service or product. But "for this customer at this time" is this the best? If not, find another match.

There is no perfect company. But for this customer at this time, are you the best? If not, refer them to the competition.

There is no perfect price. But do you have the best value?

And you don't have to be the best salesperson in the world, the nation, the state, or the city. Not even the best salesperson in the company. But for this customer, at this time, are you the best? If not, refer her to another salesperson within your organization. I'm a believer in what goes around, comes around.

You may not want to hear this

A sales manager in Washington, D.C. was typical of several seminar attendees who have told me similar stories.

"I've been wrestling with some uneasiness at my job," he began. "Now I see why. I don't believe in what I'm doing. I don't believe in our management or the way they deal with our customers. I think I've got a problem. What would you do in my situation?"

I asked how much influence he had as far as making changes at the company.

"None."

Do you see any change or hope on the horizon?

"No."

I told the sales manager that if he really wanted my opinion, I'd give it to him. But don't ask if you don't want to hear it. And please don't tell your owner who paid the money for you to attend my seminar. He's not going to be happy about this.

When you believe in what you're doing, you're confident. You do things confident people do. When you're not confident, you're indecisive, tentative, and not inspiring to others.

Would you rather be in a sinking boat with someone who believed he could save you, or with someone who expressed doubts about your survival? Believe in what you're doing or bail out and make room for those who do.

Belief is a thought. Confidence is a thought. You create your own thoughts. What *are* you thinking?

28

Famous Quotes

Did the Three Stooges Ever Reject a Script?

 "I saw this guy hitchhiking with a sign that said 'Heaven.' So I hit him." – Steven Wright.

"Be prepared." – Boy Scout motto.

"Huh? What happened?" – Every salesperson after another bombed presentation.

Ask any staffing consultant and they'll tell you to prepare for every job interview. Your future's at stake. Don't do anything stupid. Don't put your foot in your mouth. Be poised. Ask the right questions.

Sales managers do ride-alongs with their salespeople to visit customers, evaluate the salesperson's skills, and see what they can do to grow the territory. I've been evaluated by sales managers. I've evaluated salespeople as a trainer.

The first time I had a ride-along manager he asked me, "What's your plan of action? What are we going to accomplish on this call?"

"Huh? You talkin' to me?" I don't know.

"Just wing it," didn't set too well with him.

"Haven't you even thought about it?" he asked.

"What's there to think about? Do our song and dance, ask for the order, and leave as happy campers."

Not the way it works. Since that first time, I've participated in numerous ride-alongs. One thing remains constant: no one – salesperson or manager – seems to know how to prepare for the meeting. "Let the chips fall where they may," seems to be the order of the day. Oh sure, we know we should prepare. But how?

My favorite quote is from Hungarian philosopher and M.D., Michael Polyani: "We know more than we know we know." But he never explained how we know what we know.

Whispered thoughts

To know what I know, I created my **Intuitive technique**. I use this for every call and every appointment I make. It's that important. The Intuitive technique shows you what you *know* – and just as importantly – what you *don't know*. When you know what you don't know, you'll then know what you're looking for. You'll be more sensitive to your environment, you'll pick up on whispered comments, and you'll see things in people's body language and how they relate to each other. Nuances that improve your odds in getting the appointments and sales.

The Intuitive technique can be used for anything in life. If you want to know what you know or don't know about your competitors, this technique works. If you want to know what you know or don't know about writing a book, this technique reveals all. If you want to know what you know or don't know about starting your own business, this technique pulls the curtain back.

If you could do anything in life

Doing our Cold Calling for Cowards® seminars, people ask how I got into the business. I never had my own company. Never did sales training. I never spoke to a larger audience of more than a dozen people during a sales presentation.

I started my business by using the Intuitive technique. I had worked for others for years, but became tired of it. I was equally tired of the corporate world. I was bored.

I called a meeting with myself. The loneliest meeting I've ever been to. I wanted to make a change in my life, but I didn't know what I wanted to do. So I got a legal pad and pen and wrote a question at the top: "If I could do anything in my life – anything – what would it be?"

Why Calculus Wasn't Fun
The more I want to get something done,
the less I call it work.

- Richard Bach

Then I started to write whatever came to mind. I wrote. And wrote. And wrote. I wrote for three days. It worried me so much that I lost five pounds. (Not a recommended weight loss plan.)

If I could do *anything*? It kept coming back to this: I'd love to do sales training seminars.

But I had a problem. I had no teaching skills. I had no background in training. I had no financial support. I had no company. I had sales skills, but no marketing skills. I had no public speaking skills. I had no books or CDs. No contacts in speakers' bureaus. No customers. Nothing.

But…I don't let small things like this stop me. I figured I was on to something.

I got another legal pad and wrote another question: "What would I do sales training on?" I answered this question with another question: "What do salespeople *hate* to do more than anything else in the selling process?"

The answer kept coming back to cold calling. Man, we hate to cold call. I would rather do anything else in sales – but cold call.

And that's how I started our seminars. Using the Intuitive technique.

Use it to prepare for appointments

Here are the seven steps for how to use the technique to prepare for your appointments and interviews.

1. Do the Intuitive technique only by yourself. No one else is to be involved. You want the security to know that everything you record will be confidential and for your eyes only. This way you'll be honest with yourself.

2. Everything must be written down (computer or longhand). You can't talk your way through it, you can't think your way through it. It must be written down. When you write it down, it focuses your attention. You'll come up with new ideas. New questions. New avenues of approach.

3. Never go back and re-write or edit anything. Leave it alone. You're trying to get everything out of your mind as quickly as your hand can empty it. Don't worry. Your brain will be able to sort everything out later.

4. You can go back and number in the margin the sequence of how you want to ask the questions. The easiest to the most

difficult. This is how you make commitment and consistency a part of your interview process.

5. Write down everything you know *or don't know.*

6. After you've finished, go back to what you don't know, do your homework, and find the answers.

7. Use this technique on every call you make. I use it on the first cold call, the first appointment, the follow-up callback, the next appointment, the closing appointment, and the delivery of the service. Every time you talk with that prospect or customer things change. You get more information. By writing it down, you can relate it to your next call.

INTUITIVE TECHNIQUE

- Prospect's name
- Objectives
- Known
- Unknown
- Questions (Exploring, Fact Finding, Sequence)
- Listen (Thoughts, Feelings, Values, Body Language)
- Next Step (Close, Appointment, Information, Eliminate)

Follow this graphic as an example of how to prepare for the call. Let's assume this is a cold call to a name you picked off a website on the Internet.

Start with the easy things first: prospect's name. Phone number. Address. Website address. Information from the About Us link. Information about their customers who give testimonials. What they sell. Their company's goals or mission. Then write down what you don't know: who influences the decision? Who's the real deci-sion-maker? How are they financed? Who are their competitors? Keep adding to this list until you run out of ideas and then go to the next item.

What are my objectives? What are their objectives? I know one objective they have is to eliminate me; they don't want to talk to another salesperson. So don't do anything stupid. Don't put my foot in my mouth. Don't interrupt. Don't ask stupid questions. Don't give them an excuse to get rid of me.

For example, a friend of mine was the gatekeeper of an organi-zation and arranged for me to visit with her president to discuss my training services. "But," she warned, "when you come over make sure your shoes are polished. The first thing she looks at are your shoes. If they're not polished, I'll guarantee you'll be out the door in fifteen minutes."

A small thing. A trivial thing. It could have cost me the sale if I hadn't prepared.

What's known, what's unknown about this prospect? Who are they doing business with now? Why? Who made the decision? What kinds of products are they using? What are they paying? What kinds of discounts are they getting? What's their employee turnover rate? What's their D&B rating?

What questions do I want to ask them, what questions do they want to ask me? I know two questions they will always ask: why should I do business with you? And why are you so expensive? They're asking you the same two questions. Why are you always surprised? Why don't you have prepared responses?

Listen. Listen to their thoughts, their values – listen to their body language. I was a ride-along with a salesman who was calling on a new client. We walked in, shook hands with the prospect, the salesman gave a solid presentation, we got up to leave, shook hands all around, and left.

Back at the car I asked the salesman, "Did you notice how the prospect shook hands with you when we met him and how he shook hands with you when we left?"

The salesman was surprised. He didn't notice the prospect shook hands two different ways coming and going. There's one handshake we'll discuss later that will change in minutes and can signal if the prospect is comfortable with you. This salesman didn't know to look for it. He wasn't prepared.

"Did you notice what the prospect did when you asked him about the money in the budget?" The salesman didn't notice.

"Did you notice what the prospect was doing with his hands when he was telling you his problems?" The salesman was clueless.

If only he'd known how to use the Intuitive technique he wouldn't have missed these valuable clues that could have won the contract.

Finally, what's my next step? Do I want to close the deal on this call? Ask for another appointment? Get more information? Give information? Do I want to eliminate this prospect from my list?

How to Become a Legend
I hated every minute of training, but I said,
"Don't quit. Suffer now and live the rest of your
life as a champion."

- Muhammad Ali

Is this a lot of work? Yes. Does it work? Yes. Do you really want to do it? How bad do you want the business?

I've always believed that salespeople and their companies must share the blame for the salesperson's lack of preparation. The salespeople haven't been taught what to look for. But now you have the Intuitive technique. No longer can you blame your company for your lack of preparation.

It's now your responsibility.

29

Your Honor, I Object!

Oh?

Dealing with objections goes a long way from turning a cold call into an appointment, an appointment into a sale.

Flying to Dallas, my seat partner was Archie, a business owner in Seattle. I asked him, "What's your best way to handle objections?"

"Oh?"

I thought he didn't hear me. "I said, what's the best way to handle an objection? I'm sure you get them all the time. Our seminar attendees are always looking for new ways to deal with this problem."

"Oh?"

"You know, in our business people have objections *du jour*. Like, 'It costs too much'. Or, 'Why can't you give us two days of training for the price of one?' Things like that."

"Oh?" Archie smiled.

Oh. I get it.

Imagine!
Vision is the art of seeing the invisible.
- Jonathan Swift

Archie explained that using the word "Oh" is the best one-word response he's ever had for dealing with objections. He said it takes the pressure off you to come up with an answer immediately and buys you time to think on your feet. By repeating it you get people to clarify and expand on their objection. You'll discover what the true objection is because it's not always the first one they bring up.

Once the customer makes it clear what's really bothering him, then you can respond to his legitimate concern. Archie said that if you try to answer every objection, people will continue throwing them out until they wear you down. He said it takes a lot of nerve to utter "Oh", but once you do you'll be amazed at how easy it is to deal with objections.

I asked him to give me an example of how he uses it.

"On one sales call this past month, the prospect said, 'Archie, your prices are too high.'"

"Oh?"

"Yeah, your competitor's price is 10% less."

"Oh?"

"Yeah. Of course the price is based on the 'X' brand rods as opposed to your 'Y' brand, but I don't see any difference between them."

"Oh?"

"Yeah, and their delivery takes about six weeks. I know you said you could have yours here by next week."

Archie said, "Look what I've done. I found out what the competition is up to. I found their price. I found we're not comparing apples to apples. And I found out they don't have inventory. All this by using the simple word, 'Oh?'".

So what did you do, I asked Archie.

"I feed his words back to him since these are the things most important to him.

"Mr. Prospect, you said their price was 10% less, but they were proposing a different product and delivery would be six weeks out. I know exactly the product they're talking about. We can get it too. But you originally said you wanted the better quality. What we proposed will last at least 20 years. What they're proposing has a life expectancy of 10 years. Now if you want that, I can get it for you. But because it is so expensive and rarely sold, we don't keep it in inventory either. It'll take us about six weeks to get it to you as well.

"So do you want a lower quality product, at a cheaper price, that will take six weeks for delivery? Or should we go with the original proposal and have it in your yard next week?"

Archie said the "Oh" rarely fails to solicit the true objection. And Archie added that if you're talking with an analytical personality, throw in the word "And", and this will go on for hours. Analyticals love to tell you how much they know.

The rise of the Phoenix

I mentioned Archie's technique in Phoenix the next month at one of our seminars. After the noon lunch break, and just before starting the afternoon session, one of the attendees rushed up to me and excitedly told me her story.

"During lunch, I took my car from the parking garage and went to meet my friend to have a salad," she said. "Returning to park my car, I showed the attendant my parking ticket. He told me the garage didn't have in-and-out parking privileges and that I'd have to pay $5 again. I didn't think that was fair, but didn't know what else to do. Then I remembered your story about Archie.

"Oh?"

"The parking attendant looked at me like I didn't hear him."

"That'll be $5 to park again," he said.

"Oh?"

"That's right. $5. To park again."

"Oh?"

"Lady, there's no in-and-out privileges here. It costs $5 to park again."

"Oh?"

Frustrated, the attendant waved her through, "Oh, go ahead and park the car lady!"

"You just saved me five bucks. Thanks."

Using "Oh" is hard for most salespeople. It's easy to say. But difficult to do. It takes a lot of nerve, but it yields big rewards.

That's Not a Problem
The solution to a problem changes the problem.
- John Peers

They're expensive

When I moved to Seattle from the Dallas/Ft. Worth area, I was selling Sony office products. They were more expensive than any of our competitors. I had a good regional manager, Mark, who said that price will be an objection that I'd face every time. He said to be prepared for it and to bring it up first.

Meeting with a doctor, I stressed that the "Sony products are *very* expensive. We have other products that are similar and are a little *cheaper*. Wouldn't you rather see one of those?"

The doctor looked at me like I had insulted his manhood. "No! I buy only the best. Show me the best you have."

Great. We just started commitment and consistency. He didn't know it, but I did. He went on record that he wanted the best. I knew it would be difficult for him to back down now.

After doing my show-n'-tell I went for the close. What do you think was his first objection? That's right. "It's too expensive."

"But doctor, don't you remember that at the very beginning I said these Sony products were expensive? But you said you buy only the best."

He smiled. Gotcha'. Got the sale.

Bank on it

Doing some preparation for on-site training with a bank, I asked one of the managers, "What are the two most common objections prospects give to your bankers when they're cold calling?"

He said that 75% of the objections are: (1) "It's too much of a hassle to change banks"; and (2) "We're doing business with someone else."

He said the bankers always seemed to be surprised every time they heard the objections and they never had a come-back response.

I asked if their bankers ever brought the objections up first. No. Because they were afraid of these two objections, they hoped they would never surface. But they did. 75% of the time. Guess they weren't going away after all.

It's been found that for every service or product, there are seven to ten objections. Knowing this, use this three step process to deal better with objections.

1. Identify the most common objections people have about your service or product. They'll use certain objections when you're cold calling, and different objections when you're closing.
2. Develop one, if not two responses to each objection.
3. Then bring up the objections first (like I did with the doctor).

For the bankers, I suggested they get out in front with statements like these.

"Ms. Business Owner, I'm sure you're doing business with another bank in town. But is there any area where we can compete for your business? For example, in lines of credit or real estate loans?"

By acknowledging that the owner's banking with someone else, her excuse has been taken away. Because her objection is immediately quashed, she doesn't have another one in the can. When the banker suggests he'll "compete" for the business, he's showing he's hungry for the business – but not desperate. And finally, by suggesting "lines of credit or real estate loans" he's identified other areas where she may have some needs.

To handle the second objection, I suggested something along these lines.

"Many small business owners tell me they'd like to change banks, but it's too much of a hassle. Our bank has been independently rated #1 on the East coast as the easiest to switch over to. It's because each banker takes personal responsibility for the migration of new accounts. Do you think we could get together for a fifteen minute discovery process to see if you'd be interested? If you are, we'll make another appointment later."

Several things are happening with this response. The "changing banks" objection has been snuffed. This stops the prospect from throwing out a knee-jerk response that has worked in the past. With the objection removed, the banker bought time to complete his thoughts.

The banker mentioned the independent #1 rating (which they did have). Doing my research in preparing for the bank's training, I found the research published on their website. But the marketing department never shared this information with the bankers to use in their sales calls. Once they became aware of it, they discovered how powerful the findings from a third party source could be.

The banker then tells the prospect how he'll make the transition hassle-free. He's taking full responsibility and will hold her hand all the way.

Finally, he asks for a fifteen minute discovery appointment to see if they're compatible. He lets her be in charge of deciding if a second appointment will be needed later.

Any objections?

So What You're Saying...
I know you believe you understand what you think I said. But I am not sure you realize that what you heard is not what I meant.

- Patrick Murray

30

How to Be #2
Until You're #1

Get Your Foot in the Door without Getting It Crushed

As mentioned earlier, Harvey Mackay - business owner, author, and speaker - said that if you can't be the #1 vendor on the prospect's list, you better be #2. Because when things change, and they will, they're not calling #3, #4, or #5. They're only calling #2.

The **Pilot Project** is one way to grab the #2 position. Assume your prospect does business with your competitor. Maybe you've found one area where the competitor is not filling a need. Maybe they don't have the service or product, or maybe it's not profitable for them. Maybe it's not even profitable for you. But you want to get your foot in the door to get a bigger piece of the pie.

Tell the prospect, "Look, here's a problem area our product could solve. But to tell you the truth, it's a low profit product; just as it's not profitable for your current vendor.

"So let's do this. You can have our product, *this one time only*, at a deeply discounted price to prove to you that we can deliver the goods. That we can do the job. If you like it and want to order more later, you can. But at the regular price that our other customers pay." (You've now protected yourself from them expecting a cheaper price on a re-order and you've justified your discount.)

"Keep your current vendor. That's fine. But this will prove that you can depend upon us if you ever get backed into a corner and need a back-up supplier."

If they agree to order, and to make the Pilot Project work, you must get money upfront for the order. Even if it's $1. Money in hand guarantees two things will happen: (a) they start using the service or product immediately – it won't sit on the shelf; and (b) they start justifying to themselves why they made the decision to buy. They start selling themselves and that takes the pressure off you.

Finally, the Pilot Project changes your relationship. No longer are they a prospect. Now they're a customer. Once they're a customer, more of your calls will be taken and returned. You'll have greater access to the decision-maker and his or her staff. And you can introduce new services and products you couldn't have otherwise.

Even for a Million Dollars
Confidence and respect are things you can't buy—you've got to earn them.
- Unknown

Steady as she goes

The next approach to position yourself to be #2 is the **Slow Approach**. I learned this my first year of selling school pictures in Dallas.

The problem with cold calling is that the salespeople lose contact with their prospects. Make the call. Not interested. Hang-up. Make the next call. Not interested. Hang-up. Repeat. Repeat. Repeat.

Here's the problem: because 95% of salespeople don't keep records on their prospects, because they don't identify the competitors the prospects are doing business with, and because they don't keep in touch, they NEVER position themselves to be #2.

And that's #2 with a Level 2 prospect. A prospect who uses their service or product from their competitor. A prospect who's going to change vendors someday. A prospect sold on the concept and has money in the budget. And the salesperson misses an opportunity to start a relationship with them.

"We've decided to do business with your competitor"

Here are two opportunities when you can implement the Slow Approach. The first occurs when you've lost the deal to the competition. Maybe your proposal was too high. Or you couldn't get the financing necessary. Don't get mad. Don't get upset. Don't go storming out the door or slam down the telephone.

Ask the prospect if you can have 5 minutes of her time to ask a couple of follow-up questions. Without taking a breath continue, "I promise not to ask for your business. I respect your decision."

She'll relax, drop her guard, and feel obligated to give you the time after all the effort you've put into the process. You really don't need 5 minutes. Even one minute makes the Slow Approach work because you've started commitment and consistency.

Honor your promise and don't ask for the business. Make sure you keep your Q&A to less than 5 minutes.

Quickly after your "I respect your decision" remark, tell her that what you want to do is position yourself to be the #2 vendor on her list.

Here's how it goes if I lose to the competition.

"Judy, I'm sorry you've decided to go with our competitor because I do feel we're the best choice; but I certainly respect your decision. I know the competitors and I'm sure they'll do a fine job.

"But…could I have 5 minutes of your time, to ask a couple of follow-up questions required by our company? I promise not to ask you for your business. What I really want to do is position myself to be the #2 vendor on your list – so just in case something happens, you'll have someone to call for help."

This shows Judy I have no hard feelings. I'm not leaving in a huffy fit or with a chip on my shoulder. I want her to know she can call me anytime something happens. I want to keep my foot in the door even if I'm on my way out the door.

You never know what will happen. I've had people call me back two or three weeks after I thought I lost the deal and I ended up getting the business. Maybe their deal fell through. Maybe they couldn't get the delivery time they wanted. Maybe the competitor made promises he couldn't keep.

"Not interested"

The second opportunity to use Slow Approach is when you're cold calling. If I'm calling and the prospect tells me he's doing business with my competitor, "Not interested," I'd respond like this.

"Oh, I know who they are. They do good work. But could I ask you two questions? And asking for your business isn't one of them. Really, what I want to do is position myself to be #2 on your list just in case you ever get in a bind and need help."

Another way I handle the cold call when I'm told "not interested" is to offer to send my business card.

"Oh, I know who they are. They do good work. But let me ask you…could I send you my business card for your files? What I really want to do is position myself to be the #2 vendor on your list so just in case you ever get in a bind you'll have someone to call."

If they agree to accept my business card, we've strengthened our commitment and consistency and they've agreed to start building a relationship with me. Not only do I have my foot in the door, but I'm leaning on the door frame and keeping #3, #4, and #5 out.

I've had sales veterans come up after our seminars and tell me what one Minneapolis business owner told me. "Jerry, you know when I started the business 25 years ago I used that technique all the time. Through the years I've forgotten about it. I'm going back to doing it."

See *Appendix C* for a program that will position you to be #2 until you're #1.

31

I'll Cut You Off at the Knees

Psychics, Psychos, and Columbo

 One of my clients in Seattle called in a panic.

"Jerry," his voice quivered, "we need your help. I think we just screwed ourselves with one of our best prospects."

Alec wanted to know if I'd come to his office ASAP to listen to a voicemail message they had saved.

Going over the next day, Alec and two of his salesmen hurried me into the conference room, shut the door, and dialed into the voicemail to retrieve the message.

"Fellas," the ominous woman's voice began, "if you try to go around me on this, I'll cut you off at the knees."

What happened?

Mum's the Word
"Shut up," he explained.

- Ring Lardner

Alec explained that the two salesmen sitting with us were working on the account in question. They had given multi-presentations and proposals, but seemed to be getting nowhere. Finally, after months of frustration, salesman #1 tried calling the company's CEO to get an appointment to get a final answer. The trigger for the voicemail.

"What can we do?" Alec asked. "The prospect is too valuable to lose. We don't want to alienate them, but the buyer sounds like she's ready to kill us. Do you think we've cut our throat? Can we save this prospect?"

Recalling a similar experience that happened to me, I suggested the following.

We'd need the help of Alec's CEO to pull this off. Would he agree? Let's see.

We pulled the CEO into the conference room to share the plan. He'd do it. The prospect was too important to do anything less.

"Okay, guys. Here's our strategy. Call your contact, the buyer, and tell her you got her message loud and clear. You're sorry you upset her and you didn't mean to. You won't go around her.

"However, when your CEO asked why, and you played back her voicemail, he got a little upset. He said he was going to call your CEO himself and get to the bottom of this.

"We tried to calm him down and told him, 'No! Don't do it!' But, 'Hey, he's the boss. I can't tell him what to do. It's his business. What can I say?'

"Then tell the buyer, 'Look. You've done a great job for us. We told our CEO so. He suggested that when he calls your boss for the meeting he'd like to have you go in with him so he can brag about you. But here's the thing. My boss is calling your boss in two hours whether you call me back or not. I hope you do, because we'd like for him to have an expert like you go into that meeting with him. So please, call me back. I'll be in the office.'"

The CEO understood exactly what I was doing, but the two salesmen who were handling the account didn't get it yet. The CEO asked me to explain.

"CEO's speak a different language than the salesmen," I told them, "different than the buyers in their cubicles. They're at a different level of communications. They're used to being direct with each other and getting to the point. They understand that's how the game's played."

I continued. "By having your CEO call her CEO, and by you protesting to your CEO not to do it, you've protected yourself for the future. If you should end up getting the account, you'll still have to work with this buyer. However, since you took her side in the situation, you're the good guys while your CEO wears the black hat. And by putting a short deadline for her to respond, you've forced her hand while still giving her a choice. She's got to either call your CEO and protest, which she won't do, or go in with your CEO."

Two hours passed. No word from the buyer. Time for our CEO to act. He called for the appointment.

"Hi, Bill. Thanks for your call," said the congenial CEO #2. "Yes, I know your two salesmen have been trying to get into our account and land the business. I've been keeping abreast of what they've been doing, and I'm impressed.

"However, there's something going on at our company they're not aware of. If you'll have them back off for about 2-3 months and then call me back, I'll make the appointment."

About six months later, Alec called and asked me to stop by for coffee. Had some good news.

Said the two salesmen called back when asked, got the appointment, and got the business. They were now booking over $10,000 per month in sales. Thanks.

I asked him for the back story of what happened.

Turns out, Alec said, the buyer had been under suspicion of doing something under the table. Maybe not illegal, but unethical at the very least. CEO #2 was aware of it and was gathering evidence to protect the company from future lawsuits. Once she was terminated, Alec's salesmen were invited in and got the business.

I asked Alec if he still had that buyer's "I'll cut you off at the knees" voicemail. Turns out he did.

"What should we do with it?"

Save it. Transfer it onto a tape or CD for posterity. Then use it for future internal sales training to show newcomers how you guys successfully handled a potentially devastating situation.

Cleared for takeoff

While at McCaw Communications, one of my largest accounts was Alaska Airlines. One day the director of purchasing called me to give me the bad news that they were canceling their account with us and going to our competitors. Nothing personal. Just a better price. The unions had been putting pressure on Alaska to cut costs, so one of the easiest areas to save money was with us.

After failing to save the account, I had my general manager go with me to try and save it again. No go. We took our vice president with us. Nothing. The account was being terminated. We were told not to bother any longer.

By a chance meeting with our company's president in Hawaii, I mentioned I was losing the account and that the GM and VP had done everything they could to save it, but to no avail.

How About This?
But above all try something.
- Franklin D. Roosevelt

"Alaska Airlines? Hmm. Tell you what Jerry, when we get back to Seattle next week give me a couple of days and then I'll call you and see if we can save this account."

Towards the end of the following week, the president called me. Had a chuckle in his voice.

"Jerry, don't worry about losing Alaska. They're yours for as long as you want them."

What happened? Our president called their president (remember they speak a different language than us). Our president reminded Alaska's how much money McCaw spent for airline tickets each year. Alaska's president didn't even know purchasing was canceling the contract. He put our president on hold, called his purchasing, and then picked up our president's line.

"Don't worry," said the Alaska prez, "you're keeping the business."

The point of the story: don't try to do everything by yourself. Get others involved. They know things, and people, you don't. Neither my GM nor the VP knew how much money McCaw spent with Alaska each year. If any of us had known, we could have used it to our advantage just as our president did.

Oh – ah – just one more thing

One technique that's worked well for me, and protected me from anyone who ever had any thoughts about cutting me off at the knees, is the **Columbo technique**. This is perhaps the best technique when you're referred down to a subordinate or to a committee.

One of the rules of sales is to try and meet with the highest level decision-maker that you can. It's not always the CEO or the President or even the General Manager. How do you find who it is?

A technique Gene, one of our Atlanta seminar attendees, told me about is to be direct. Look on the company's website and find the name of the highest ranking person listed. Then call and ask for her.

When the gatekeeper asks him, "Will she know who you are and what this is about?" he always answers, "Not unless she's a psychic." He said the gatekeeper always laughs and usually puts him through.

Here's to You Mrs. Robinson
Life is largely a process of seduction. You must seduce favors and chances for achievement out of people. It's not strange that the same tools required for love should be required for success in any field.

- Ben Stein

Or you can take the advice of my New York friend who used to be the executive assistant for the CEO of a Fortune 500 company.

She said that if you're doing a cold call, especially to a large company, don't try and get through to the CEO. They don't take calls like this. That's why they hire gatekeepers. My friend said that when you call, ask to speak with the executive assistant to the CEO or president. They're required to take calls.

She said to be upfront with the assistants, tell them what you want, and if necessary direct her to a website or send information for her to look at to decide if anyone in her company would be interested. She said that since she's been with the CEO for over 20 years, she knows his every needs, quirks, and schedule. She knows everyone in the company.

My friend would then tell the salesperson something like this. "You know, our CEO doesn't handle that. But we have a vice president of operations in Connecticut who might be interested. If you'd like I can give you his number."

Get permission to use the executive assistant's name as the person who referred you.

I've found a lot of business with her advice. But then I throw in the Columbo twist when I meet the decision-maker; especially if I know this is going to be a selling cycle that will take a month or two.

Walking in to shake hands with the vice president, I remain standing. "Thanks for seeing me and I won't be more that a couple of minutes. What I'd like for you to do is refer me down to someone who takes care of the details on a service like this so I can explain it to them without taking your time. If they're interested, I'm sure I'll be back to see you again. Would that be okay?"

You bet! He doesn't have to meet with another salesman. Besides, he's not a detail guy. That's why he hired the others.

"Be glad to Jerry. You need to see Betsy. She's in charge of our training. Here. Here's her extension."

"Thanks," I say, taking the card, "but would you do me a favor? Would you call down and see if she's available now? Would you give me a quick telephone introduction so she knows I'm coming?"

With the VP calling, I have more clout. The training manager doesn't know how well I know the VP and if he asks a favor, she knows to grant it. And a personal introduction is one of the best ways to connect.

She's in. The VP introduces me and is ready to send me down. We shake hands once again. He circles his desk and sits down as I'm walking out. "Good, got rid of another salesman," he's thinking as he relaxes.

Hand on the doorknob, I slowly turn around to face the VP whose head is buried in his paperwork. Placing my index finger to my lips I say, "Oh. By the way. If you don't mind, I'd like to keep you in the loop so you'll know what's going on. Will it be okay to drop you an email or leave you a voicemail as to what the progress is? You won't ever need to respond."

"Sure," he replies. Decision-makers like to be kept in the loop, especially if they don't have to talk with you.

"Great. I'll get your business card and email address from your assistant on the way out."

Great. See ya' buddy.

I turn to leave again. I'm half-way out the door, he's half-way through is notes.

"Oh. One more thing. Just in case we should get bogged down later on in any details, can I come back to you for advice as to what we should do?"

Using commitment and consistency once again, I've been able to keep my foot in the door. Because the VP has agreed to let me get this deep into his organization, he's got to be consistent with all his responses. I now have access to him whenever I want. Now the trainer, gatekeeper, or anyone else can't say, "I'll cut you off at the knees if you try to go around me." I'm telling them upfront that I have access to the VP whenever I want and that I will be keeping in touch with him via email and voicemail as to our progress. All threats vanish.

"Sure, sure. No problem," the VP responds. "Just let me know how I can help."

We've cemented commitment and consistency. He's agreed to help if things hit the wall.

I bid adieu again. I stop by the assistant's desk as I'm leaving and tell her that the VP said I could get one of his business cards and email address. In like Flint.

Dropping in to the trainer's office downstairs, I tell her about the wonderful meeting I had with her boss, and that he gave me his email address so I could keep him in the loop of our discussions. She now knows I have access. She knows not to threaten me when things get bogged down (and they will).

Guess what? After six months, nothing is happening. Molasses moves faster. We're bogged down. I pick up the phone to call the VP. I haven't seen him for the past six months, but I have been sending him regular updates. He knows who I am. I remind him of our earlier conversation.

"You know, as I was leaving your office I asked that if we get bogged down, could I come back to you for advice. Well…we're stuck. What would you suggest I do?"

Because of the power of commitment and consistency (there is no deadline for it – it could go on for years), and because I reminded him of our conversation and his agreement, I'll get the help I need. It's never failed me yet.

32

I'll Get Back to You

And Other Fairy Tales

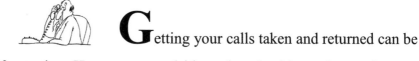etting your calls taken and returned can be frustrating. Here are several ideas shared with me by seminar attendees that have been successful for them. I've used them all, and they definitely work for me.

Fork technique

Doing a training session in Nebraska, I met one of the top saleswomen for her company during a break. I asked her, "What's your secret for getting your calls taken and returned?"

"Easy," she said, with a twinkle in her eyes. She found the idea in the book, *I'll Get Back to You: 156 Ways to Get People to Return Your Calls and Other Helpful Tips*, by Eric Yaverbaum and Robert L. Shook. "I send the decision-maker a fork with a note attached to it."

What's on the note?

"The note, written on the back of my business card, says, 'This fork is to remind you that you *fork-got* to call me back…don't make me come after you with a *knife*!'"

She said that when she calls to follow-up the next week, the secretary says, "Who can I say is calling?"

"Tell your boss it's the lady who sent him the fork."

She said they always laugh because that fork has been sent around to everyone in the office. If the head honcho is there, she gets put through.

Is That a Monet?
Somebody once did a painting of our sales department. It was a still life.

- Unknown

Cheese technique

During one of my Dallas seminars I asked the group, "How do you get an appointment with someone who won't take your calls? Someone who doesn't want to change from their current vendor?"

During our morning break, a very professional young woman came up to me and said, "My office is nearby. During the noon hour I'll run over and get something to show you how we do it."

Before starting our afternoon session, she took me aside and handed me a copy of Spencer Johnson's and Kenneth Blanchard's *Who Moved My Cheese? An Amazing Way to Deal with Change in Your Work and in Your Life*. The long-time best selling book is about change – and what will happen if you don't.

The Dallas professional said they buy the books by the carton directly from the publisher. Then each sales rep writes inside the cover, "This book only takes an hour to read. Hope you enjoy it. I'll call next week to see what you think about it."

She said they have been getting so many first-time appointments with the cheese technique that it has increased their sales tremendously.

A note of caution. In San Francisco, the CEO of a medium sized company approached me during a break and asked what I thought about his idea.

One of his two best customers had a new CEO. He hadn't met with him yet and kept getting put on the back burner. The San Francisco CEO said he had purchased a beautiful leather briefcase that cost over $300 as a gift for the new CEO. Said his secretary had just wrapped it this morning and FedEx was scheduled to pick it up that afternoon for delivery. What did I think about that idea?

"I'm not sure what your business is, or how gifts are perceived by your customer," I said. "I have heard some companies say that they would consider this as a type of bribe. So I'd be very cautious sending something this expensive.

"But if you still want to send it, why not attach a note with a thought like this: 'Congratulations as the new CEO of the X Company. Your company has been our best customer for the last five years and I hope the tradition continues. I'd like to present this welcoming gift to you, but would understand if you can't accept it. If not, please feel free to donate it to your favorite charity. I'll call next week to see if we can get together for lunch.'"

"Whew!" my new friend said. "You may have saved me from making a major *faux pas*. I'll call the office now and have my secretary hold it until I can put the note inside."

Simple technique

Simply ask. This is the easiest way to get your calls returned, but the most overlooked. When you ask, and they answer, you've started commitment and consistency.

"Will you call me back next Tuesday morning at 10?"

"You bet Jerry. Be glad to."

"Great," I respond, "I'll mark it in my calendar and hope you mark it in yours as well."

But then I put a twist on it. I take the initiative back away from the customer. Instead of depending upon him to call me, I'll say, "You know, every once in awhile I may get called out to a meeting. Just in case I miss your call, would it be okay if I call you back that afternoon?"

He can't say no. He's already committed to talk with me. Besides, he's thinking I'm like 95% of other salespeople: I won't remember and I won't call back. But guess what? I'm not. I'm a 5%er. I do what 95% of other salespeople won't do. I make a note, and I'll call back.

Next Tuesday gets here. 10 a.m. No call. 10:15. No call. 11 a.m. No call.

That afternoon, I'm on the phone calling him. But I don't want to embarrass him. I'll start the conversation with, "You know we talked last week and you were going to call me back this morning. I'm sorry, but I was in a meeting (I wasn't but this is where the face saving comes in) and must have missed your call. But you said it would be okay to call you back this afternoon." Well, here-e-e's Jerry.

Mission Impossible
I told my boy that nothing is impossible. He said: "Let's see you gargle with your mouth shut."

- Unknown

Law of Reciprocation technique

Learn to use the Law of Reciprocation to get your calls returned. The Law of Reciprocation works two ways: (1) if a favor is given and received, the recipient is obligated at a future date to return the favor; or (2) if a concession is made by one party, the other party is obligated to return a concession.

Let's use the first technique to get your calls returned. Give a favor. Two of the most popular ways to give a favor is to give of your time, or to give an idea.

Salespeople don't realize that when they give of their time, even if it's one minute answering a question, they have the right to ask for something in return. And what they want is a call back. They've earned the right to ask for it.

The second way to give a favor is to give an idea. But make the idea something they can use now. Something that will produce dramatic, measurable, short-term results, using the resources they have available, and using the authority they have now.

Such an idea is the **Negotiating for Discount technique**. Tell your customer, just before hanging up, "You know we attended a seminar last week and we found how your salespeople can stop leaving your company's money on the table when they're asked for a discount. Would you like to hear it?"

You bet I would. It's my money. I want to keep it.

"Okay, here's what you do. When the salesperson is pressed for a discount, he must ask for something in return. And what he wants are three referrals."

What do you mean?

"I need a 15% discount," the customer demands.

The salesperson calmly replies, "15%? I don't know. I'll have to call my sales manager to get her approval. She might do it, but I don't know. But if she says okay, she's going to ask for something in return. And what she wants in return are the names of three buyers you know who could use our services who you'd give us a referral to. How's that sound?"

"Look what you did with this technique," you tell your customer. "You stopped the buyer from nickel-and-diming you to death. Now he knows that if he asks for another concession, you're also going to ask for something in return.

"And you've also placed value on the discount. No longer is it just a freebie you pulled from out of the air. Now it's worth something. It cost him the names of three friends. This discount means something to him now."

And then you add, "Oh, by the way, could you give me a call next Thursday afternoon?" Give a favor, ask for a favor.

Later
To make a long story short...there's nothing like having the boss walk in.
- Unknown

Another good idea you can exchange for a call back?

I was doing some training for one of the world's largest chemical companies based in St. Louis. During one of the breaks the president came over, pulled me aside, and whispered to me, "One word."

Excuse me?

"One word," the president said. "If you're such a great trainer, give me one word that will make a difference in getting better results."

"Oh, that's easy," I said. "*Because.* That's the word." I explained to him how it works. "I'll send you a copy of Robert Cialdini's book, *Influence: the Power of Persuasion*, and I'll mark the chapter where he talks about the psychology of the word *because.*"

About three weeks later I got a nice handwritten thank you note from the president. "Jerry – that word 'because' is dynamite! It really works. Thanks."

Here's how the ***Because* technique** works. Just before hanging up the phone and before asking for the call back, tell the customer you saw a good idea for getting that salesperson who's always late for meetings to show up on time. Want to hear it?

"Of course!"

"Okay, do this. Make your request and just before you give the reason for it, throw in the word *because.* Harvard psychologist Ellen Langer found that people like to have reasons if you ask them for a favor. The magic of *because*, she said, is that the reason doesn't even have to be real. She said people are programmed to accept the explanation as valid if it follows the word *because.*

"For example, 'Tim, I need you to be on time for the sales meeting tomorrow at 8 a.m. *because* I've got to be at headquarters at 9.' Or, '...*because* I've got to wash my car at the Pink Elephant.' Or, '...*because* we're having a full moon tomorrow night.'

"Dr. Langer said that for some strange reason, once the mind hears *because*, it switches off and accepts what preceded it as the only valid information to be processed.

"By the way," you continue, "could you give me a call back Friday morning?"

Give a favor, ask for a favor. It's your right. And the Law of Reciprocation makes it work.

P.S. I have found one flaw with Dr. Langer's use of the word *because*. It doesn't seem to work with kids of any age.

Just So You Know technique

Author and psychologist Dr. David J. Lieberman, *Get Anyone to Do Anything – and Never Feel Powerless Again*, says you need to get someone to develop a sense of obligation so that if she fails to do something as promised it will cause a disturbance for you. This makes others have to care about their actions and puts their reputation on the line. This changes the equation of the call and gives you leverage.

Scene: the customer's agreed to call you back next Tuesday at 9:30. Now firm up the commitment.

"I look forward to your call on Tuesday. I do have another appointment at that time, but because your call is important to me, I know my friend will let me re-schedule. I'm sure you're busy, too, so will you be okay in keeping the 9:30 telephone appointment?"

Once she's committed, she's committed. She's gone on record. You've given her a chance to back out so you can re-schedule if need be. And because she's "putting you out" of having to re-do your schedule, you've solidified the chance of getting the call.

Without knowing it, I used this technique to get my first sales job. Interviewing with the franchise owner over coffee at a restaurant on the North Central Expressway in Dallas, I got up to leave after what I thought was a good 30-minute meeting. For some unexplained reason, as we were standing there getting ready to go our separate ways, I shook the owner's hand and said, "Just so you know – I'm interested in you. Are you interested in me?"

"Yes I am," he replied. (There's that commitment and consistency thing again.)

After working with the company for a year, the franchise owner asked me if I knew why I got the job. I was curious. No, I didn't.

He said, "Do you remember when you got up from the interview, shook my hand, and said, 'I'm interested in you – are you interested in me?'"

Of course.

"That's why you got the job. I had the position narrowed down to three people. But you were the only one to ask me for the job. That's why you got it."

Just so you know.

Skeletons in the Closet technique

Use humor to get your calls returned. Lighten up. Every call is not that important. Humor works if you know your customer likes to laugh as well.

Archie McPhee's in Seattle is the best novelty shop on the West coast. That's where I get my rubber chickens, among some of my other props.

I could never get the sales manager of a Fortune 500 company to return my call after she had my proposal. Knowing she had a weird sense of humor, and having nothing to lose, I went to McPhee's and purchased an 18" rubber skeleton, attached a note to it, and mailed it to her.

When she pulled out the skeleton, she saw my note: "This is me. Waiting for you. To return my call."

She called me that day and I got her business.

So, go ahead. See what skeletons your customers have in their closets.

Make It a Shiner Bock
A skeleton walks into a bar and says, "Give me a beer and a mop."

- Willie Nelson

Now that – folks – is a stalker

What's the difference between being persistent and being a stalker?

People who are persistent keep asking until they get an answer. Not only will they accept a "No!" they'll encourage it so everyone can get on with his life.

But as long as the prospect wants to keep the lines of communication open, you've got to keep in touch. Remember, you could be dealing with the Analytical decision-maker. It takes them 5-7 calls to move to the next step. And 5-7 for the next. They represent a lo-o-o-ng selling cycle.

If you're afraid of being a pest, be candid. "I want to be persistent. I don't like giving up. But I don't want to wear out my welcome either. I'll leave it up to you. Would you like for me to keep in touch, or should I move on?"

Almost always they're apologetic and will ask you to hang in there. They just can't make quick decisions.

What's a stalker? You can tell them "NO!" until you're blue in the face, and they still come after you. They never give up.

A lady in Dallas, Pecan, is my haunting reminder. She never attended our seminar, but she did buy one of my CD's. She called me after listening to it and had a question about getting a prospect to call her back. He never would after many attempts on her part.

I asked Pecan where they stood at this point of the relationship.

"Well," she began, "on my last call he told me to stop calling. He said he thought I was a stalker, that I scared him, and to never call him again."

Uh-oh.

"Why do you keep calling him then?" I asked. "He's given you an answer."

She hesitated. "Well...uh...I think I'm infatuated with him. I know he's married, but I don't care. What should I do?"

"DON'T CALL HIM BACK!" Get a life lady. Move on.

Pecan wasn't happy with my response, but she finally got off the phone.

Called me back the next day. "Jerry, he's REALLY mad at me now! I didn't do what you said and I called him back anyway. What can I do to get him to return my call?"

Wait a minute. You want me to give you advice for how to stalk a guy? I'm too pretty to go to prison.

"Pecan. Never call him again or the police will be taking you to the nearest calaboose in Dallas. And never call me back either."

There, that did it.

Two years later, I'm going to Dallas to do my seminar at the Omni in Richardson. Somehow Pecan had received one of our brochures and knew I was coming to town. Or maybe she was stalking our website to see my schedule. Anyway, she had been trying to call me, but I wouldn't take her calls. I was afraid she'd sign up for the seminar. She didn't. Good. I could relax. When checking into the hotel the day before the seminar, I told the clerk at the front desk Pecan's name and that if she called not to put her through.

Getting to my room the next evening at the end a long seminar day, I flopped down onto my bed. R-r-r-i-i-i-g. Picking up the phone, I was shocked to hear the voice.

"Jerry," Pecan pleaded, "I know you've just finished your seminar and you're probably tired. But I'm down here in the lobby. Could you please come down and give me some advice for how I can get my (same) prospect to return my calls? I'm really getting desperate."

And I'm getting really scared.

Now that – folks – is a stalker.

And no. I didn't go down. And no. I never saw her or talked with her again. I only hope the guy she's stalking is safe as well.

Then Getting on with Your Life
Intelligence is quickness in seeing things as they are.

- George Santayana

33

30 Seconds to Crash and Burn

Lights! Camera! Action!!

Prospects see your company and competitors like they see fingerprints: they all look the same.

Yet your fingerprints are invisible, they last, and they're yours. Each contact you make, every voicemail you leave, and every call you don't return leaves an impression. What impressions are you leaving behind?

Our job as salespeople is to be the fingerprint experts and show customers what makes us different from the pack.

Harry Beckwith, *Selling the Invisible: A Field Guide to Modern Marketing*, said that to the untrained eye we all look alike. If the customer can't tell us apart from the competition, they start looking at the trivial things to eliminate us. They're not looking for reasons to do business with us. They're looking for reasons to not even talk with us. Did you show up on time? Did you follow-up with the brochure? Are your shoes polished? Don't do stupid things that get you eliminated.

One way to help your cause and distinguish yourself from the competition is to develop several good 30-second commercials. Some you'll use on the phone. Others will be delivered in person.

Red-Headed Stranger

In Nashville, we were taught that the shorter you can make a song and still get your point across, the better the chances of airplay.
                                          - Willie Nelson

Telephone 30-second commercial

The concept of a good 30-second phone commercial is to state what you can do better than the competition – and prove it. On the phone, in thirty seconds, give your name, your company name, make a statement about a common problem that exists in the market today, and tell how your service or product can solve that problem.

For example, when I cold call on the phone to promote our sales training seminar, my 30-second commercial may go like this:

> *Hi. This is Jerry Hocutt with Hocutt & Associates. You know, most salespeople say they don't have the time to cold call. I can show you how to get your salespeople to make 3800 cold calls this year, spending less than six minutes a day. Want to hear it?*

The common problem? Sales managers can't get their salespeople to cold call. I have a solution. It's measurable and it has quantifiable results: they can make 3800 cold calls this year, spending less than six minutes a day.

By asking if they'd like to hear my solution, I'm qualifying the prospect. If they're interested, I may have a suspect. If they have no interest, I'll move on.

Face-to-face commercial

An in-person 30-second commercial is different. Instead of stating a problem and offering a solution, I'll do more questioning or offer them something free that can improve their sales. You can do this if you're networking, working trade shows, or doing walk-in calls.

For example, at chamber breakfasts or luncheons they'll bring in a keynote speaker. When the speaker is finished, they'll often go around the room and allow members to stand up, introduce themselves, and do a quick 30-second commercial. I've seen members blow a fantastic opportunity to market and advertise themselves. They'll stand up, make a feeble attempt at humor, mumble something, and sit down. And no one has any idea what that person does for a living.

Instead of risking embarrassment, create a good 30-second commercial you'll repeat verbatim at every chamber meeting for the next year. You want the other members to remember it so well they'll be able to lip sync with you.

My 30-second commercial sounds like this.

> *Hi, I'm Jerry. We have two free services your sales-people can start using today to get them in front of customers. If you're interested, please see me after the program and they're yours.*

This commercial is informal since we're face-to-face. My first name is sufficient. Don't need my company name. We'll get there if they're interested. I've identified a problem: their salespeople need to see more customers. I have a solution: two free services that will help them get in front of buyers to increase their sales.

My chamber commercial attracts people to me like a magnet.

I wouldn't use this script on the telephone since we don't have face-to-face contact. On the phone I want to give them my full name so they won't think this is a con. Since they can't see me, giving my full name helps to create trust. I also give my company name; they feel I must be legit since someone trusted me enough to hire me.

Opportunity Talking
A message without a specific request is a wasted opportunity.

- Milo O. Frank

Walk-in cold call commercial

Here's another 30-second commercial I developed while doing 45 – 70 walk-in cold calls a day at McCaw Communications that continues to be my bread and butter today. This shows you how fast the commercial goes and how quickly I can qualify or disqualify a prospect.

> *Hi. I was talking with your neighbors next door about how our pagers can be used by their sales and service departments to increase their sales. Does your company use pagers?*

Since I was talking with their neighbors next door (or down the street or in the building) they don't know if the neighbor is a customer of mine or not. Talking to their neighbors "gave me the right" to be in the area and to stop in and see them. I stated a benefit: increase their sales through their sales and service departments. By asking if they use pagers now, I qualify them by discovering if they're a Level 2 prospect (use my product from my competitor) or Level 3 (don't use pagers from anyone).

And here's a little trick I discovered to take the pressure off you and the person you've just walked in on. As I approach the receptionist, I have a pager in my hand, hold it up, and point to it. They see what I'm talking about. By directing their gaze (follow my finger) from me to the product, they don't feel obligated to make eye contact. As they're looking at what's in my hand, I'm checking out their body language, I see who else is in the area, and I can scan the environment to see what kinds of office equipment they have. It's a clue to see if they're spending money to update their business or not. If you don't have a product with you, handing them a brochure, business card, or free promotional pen will do just as well.

I made the pager-in-hand approach on one company, and as I was giving my opening line, I noticed several people standing behind the counter talking. I raised my voice slightly as I continued. The gatekeeper said they were happy with their current vendor but I could leave a brochure. (I always recommend leaving something behind, even if it's a business card. It's your visible fingerprint. Sure it may get thrown away, but there's a chance it could fall into the right person's lap.)

I left my card, took a company card from the receptionist's desk and walked outside. I used to never ask for a business card from my prospects until Rose Marie, a saleswoman I worked with and respected, scolded me for it.

"*Always* get their business card," she said. "It has the correct spelling of the company's name, often it's the card of a decision-maker with their name and correct spelling, you'll have the street address, mailing address, and vital phone numbers – many are direct numbers. Plus, the quality of the card and the logo design will be a clue about the company – do they do things on the cheap or with class?" She was right. Business cards are full of valuable clues when you know what you're looking for. They'll even include website, email, and blog addresses.

Back to the story. Standing on the prospect's sidewalk, I flipped their business card over and made a quick note of who they were doing business with. They're a Level 2 prospect for sure. File it. Things change. Even doing 45-70 walk-in calls each day I kept records on every single contact. Identifying prospects, keeping records, and keeping in touch is how I became #1 in the nation.

As I was recording the information, I felt a tap on my shoulder. Turning around, the man handed me his business card.

"I'm the president of the company you just called on. Call me next week and set an appointment. I overheard you talking with my receptionist, and we are interested in changing communication companies. She just didn't know it."

I got his business the next week.

Trade show commercial

Here's another 30-second commercial that I've used at trade shows when calling on fellow exhibitors during the breaks.

Hi, I'm Jerry. Do you have trouble getting your salespeople to follow-up their show leads? Are they as persistent as you wish they'd be?

Two questions about problems managers have in the aftermath of trade shows. 86% of leads are never followed-up. And if salespeople do follow-up, they stop after two contacts. But it takes a minimum of five contacts to round first base and head into second. They're quitting too soon and their sales managers don't have a tool to help them to be persistent. We do. But I don't offer my solution yet. I'm waiting for their response to qualify or disqualify them. If they say it's a problem, then I'll reveal the solution. (Go to www.YouveGotContacts.com to get your own persistency tool.)

Get yourself a pack of 30-second commercials in the can. Make sure they don't go beyond the thirty seconds. The shorter the better. Remember the advice from Red-Headed Stranger.

5-4-3-2-1 – You're On!

34

Good to See You Again...eh...Bill? Bob? John? Shirley?

Nuts! How to Remember Names Better

Isn't it embarrassing to walk into a sales presentation when you thought you were meeting with only the president but then found she also invited her sales manager, office manager, service manager, and bookkeeper to attend as well?

She introduced everyone all around. But you do your entire presentation – and exit – without calling any of them by name because you couldn't remember them. Wouldn't you have made them feel more important if you could have recalled their names? Won't your competitor make a better impression coming in on your heels if he does?

Some of the best sales advice I ever got was from Bob Burg, *Endless Referrals: Network Your Everyday Contacts into Sales.*

Doing a seminar in Seattle he said that, "If you're going to be in business, if you're going to be in sales, or if you're going to do public speaking, I'd highly recommend that you learn how to remember people's names."

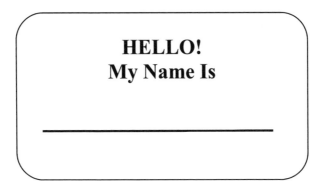

Bob said he could go to an after-seminar networking function and people would come over to him and challenge him to remember their names. He said he was like a flame to a moth.

John F. Kennedy, Jr. is legendary for remembering names. He could attend a packed banquet, make the rounds of all the tables, meet the guests, and recall everyone's name. How impressed were those who felt important enough for a celebrity like Kennedy to remember them?

Harry Lorayne, *Remembering People: the Key to Success*, and the great memory expert, found that one of the highest rated talents you can have in business is the ability to remember names. And one of the most damaging attributes that causes more lost sales is the inability to remember names. He also found that 41% of people taking memory courses do so in order to learn how to remember names. The next highest percentage, 15%, attended because they wanted to learn better in school or business.

Become a name magician

I'm certainly no expert in remembering names; I struggle just like everyone else. But I have my days. Doing seminars across the country to general audiences, I'd work the room before the program got started meeting as many attendees as I could. I'd meet more during the breaks. Then throughout the program I'd call them by name to ask or answer questions.

Hello? Who is this?
Names are important. Without them, the
phone book would just be a book of numbers.
- Unknown

What surprised me was their amazement that I could remember so many names. They made me feel like a name magician. We would have 300-500 attendees at each seminar and the ones I met I never forgot. Remember other people's names so they won't forget yours.

Had a group attend our Orlando seminar that came back after our lunch break. The president of the company asked to speak with me before the program got started again.

"Jerry, I have a group of eight people here today. We're really enjoying your seminar and we're getting a lot of great tools from it. But one thing dominated our lunch today. How in the world do you remember so many people's names?!"

I never told anyone how I did it because I didn't need the added pressure. It's sure to happen (although it hasn't yet – knock on wood) that I'll tell someone I can remember names and then my mind goes completely blank.

But because so many people kept asking me and my staff how I did it, I started sharing my secret. Keep in mind that if we ever meet, I'm strictly an amateur at this. I'm nothing like the pros Bob Burg or Harry Lorayne.

One of my favorite song titles is from Elvis Presley's last single for Sun Records, *I Forgot to Remember to Forget (You)*. The sad thing is I remember when it came out.

Why can we remember someone's face, but not their name?

What's going on? It's because remembering names is a recall function. Remembering faces is a recognition function. Both use different parts of the brain. It's easier to recognize a face than it is to recall a name.

Remember the last time you checked in to a hotel? The desk clerk called you by your name. You call down to room service and they call you by your name. The operator calls you with a message and she calls you by your name. Know where that came from?

Years ago, the Westin Hotels found they could improve the ratings of their hotels by their guests by 25% by simply calling them by their names. Their ratings increase didn't require any capital expenditures or anything high tech. Just calling their guests by their names.

Story of My Life
After a certain number of years, our faces become our biographies.
> *- Cynthia Ozick*

Okay, so what's my secret?

Five things you can to do to remember names better:

1. Make sure you *hear* the name first. The single biggest reason we "forget" names is because we never heard it to begin with. Before the start of the seminar I'll meet as many of my guests as possible. I'll walk over and shake their hands and say, "Hi, I'm Jerry." They almost always respond by saying their name. Because I know they'll do this, I have my ears perked up and pay attention. I won't let others or the surroundings distract me. I'm completely focused on hearing their name.

   If they shake my hand, but don't say their name, I'll say, "Sorry. I didn't catch your name." They'll give it up now. Or if they say their name, and I don't catch it, I'll hold the handshake for a second or two longer, step into them and say, "Sorry. I didn't hear your name. Could you repeat it (or spell it) for me?" Does it upset people for me to ask for the name? No way. They're thrilled to think that I would think they're important enough to learn their name. And they are that important to me.

   I don't use the old technique of repeating their name three or four times during our short conversation as it annoys them and it becomes patronizing. I will repeat their name when they say it. Converse. Shake hands as I depart. If I temporarily forgot their name, or if it's an unusual name, when I shake hands to leave, I'll use their name again. "Kathryn? With a K? Is that right?" Now I've got it.

2. The next step is to create *picture* cues. If I meet a Michael, I immediately see my brother Mike standing next to him with his arm around Michael's shoulders. And since he said Michael and not Mike (Michael is more formal), I see both

of them in tuxedos. Then I create another picture cue. My brother lives in Chicago. I see the two Michaels standing together with the Sears Tower and Chicago skyline behind them. Finally, a third picture. I see a microphone (mic) on Michael's shoulder in a tiny tuxedo. The pictures and name are ingrained.

Usually these two steps are enough to get the job done. In most business situations today, knowing the person's first name is acceptable. But if you want to challenge yourself, use steps three and four to learn their last name.

3. Spell the person's last name silently. Michael Rotella has an unusual last name I've never heard before. I start spelling it slowly to myself: R – o – t – e. And then I stop. I've got it. Rotella reminds me of a garden *rototiller*. The picture just has to remind me of the name. The *true* memory remembers the name correctly. As I'm looking at Michael, I see him plowing the carpets of the seminar room with his rototiller and everyone is getting upset and screaming at him to stop. And since his first name is Michael, I see millions of tiny microphones dressed in tuxedos flying up from the ground. The sillier you can make the picture the better your chance to remember it.

4. Make the *face* give up the name. This causes you to really pay attention to the people you meet. I found this great book by attorney and jury consultant Mac Fulfer called *Amazing Face Reading: An Illustrated Encyclopedia for Reading Faces*. I bought the book for the purpose of learning how to identify different facial features on people in order to use them to remember names better. But it turned out

to be an even more interesting book by showing what the size of your nose, or ears, or eyes say about you.

How do you make the face give up the name? Let's say you're meeting Katie Couric, the CBS news anchor and former Today Show host. The irises of her eyes are so large they leave little white showing. Means she's a visual learner. The picture I'd create of her last name would be a doctor *curing* her large eyes. The name and picture don't have to be exact, as long as they remind me of her name. Julia Roberts has a wide mouth and full lips. My picture of her last name would be someone must have *robbed* another's lips to add to hers. I think you get the picture.

5. The last step is to use television or the movies to practice. As you watch the program unfold, learn every character's name. When you get really good, learn the actor or actress who's playing the character and then remember both names. When we travel, I like to watch the local news stations and learn the names of the anchors, reporters, and people they're interviewing. Then at the end of the newscast I try to recall each person's name in the order they appeared.

Remember That Fork in the Road?

A good rule of thumb is if you've made it to thirty-five and your job still requires you to wear a name tag, you've probably made a serious vocational error.

- Dennis Miller

How long does it take to do all this? Believe it or not, about 2-4 seconds once you get it down. It will be a little hard at first, but once you get the hang of it, it's fun.

At a seminar in Tacoma, Washington, we had a contest. I would give $20 to the person who could remember the most names of the other attendees in 10 minutes. The man who won learned more than triple the number of names than anyone else. Handing him his $20, I asked how he got to be so good at learning names. "I wait tables. I take orders without writing them down. Learning names is a piece of cake."

Is it important to learn how to remember names? Money's riding on it.

35

Mirror, Mirror on the Wall

Hell's Angels

One of the fastest ways to create a good first impression and improve rapport is to use the mirror image. People will think you're reading their mind.

Why use the mirror image? Why do people like looking in a mirror?

We usually mirror unconsciously. Ever see a yawn become contagious? If you smile at someone, don't they smile back? If your foot taps to the music, aren't they dancing with you?

Put it to practical use

If you're calling on a customer and she says she's getting a cup of coffee, "Would you like one too?" what would you say?

Even if you don't like coffee tell her to "Make mine black." You don't have to drink it. The fact that you're mirroring her gets you off on the right foot.

If the prospect leans forward to speak, lean forward to listen. It's not as obvious as you think. You'll probably do it naturally anyway. But sometimes you may find yourself in a difficult or defensive situation and start to withdraw or show insecurity. You'll notice you may have crossed your arms or legs. Maybe you've turned slightly away from the customer. This is when you need to be aware of what you're doing, stop, and continue mirroring again.

Two part technique

Most people are aware of the first part of the mirror image: to follow the other person's gestures. But they're not aware of the second part: at some point, you want to stop following and start leading.

After mirroring the customer with her drink, with her small talk, with her gestures of sitting back and relaxing, make a decision to start creating your own gestures and see if she follows. If she does, you have control of the situation. Now she begins to follow.

Pity Those Who Don't Read
In cryptology, that's called a "self-authorizing language". That is, if you're smart enough to read it, you're permitted to know what is being said.
- The Da Vinci Code

If you're presenting your product, place it on her desk, lean forward and touch it. See if she does the same. Maybe mention what the product has done for others and see if she mirrors your statement with an example of her own or stories she's heard from others.

One favorite mirroring technique many salespeople like is the pen-to-paper technique. If you're showing a brochure, or even if you're bringing out the contract to be signed, move the tip of the pen to the area to which you want to draw attention. On the contract maybe you want her eyes to move towards the area for her signature. By moving the pen to the bottom of the contract and following it with your eyes, chances are she'll meet you at the dotted line. By stating, "All I need is your autograph here," and then tilting your pen in her direction, she'll take the pen and give you the business.

Is the mirroring technique deceitful? Is it deceitful if you're having an important lunch and choose to wear your power suit instead of a tank top? Is it deceitful if you're a woman who puts on her make-up before going to work? Is it deceitful if you're nervous before doing a presentation but put on a brave face?

You mirror others every day without knowing it. When you talk to your kindergartner, don't you get down to his level, use the same words he uses, and use the same exaggerated gestures? Does he feel like he's being manipulated; or does he feel that you understand him?

When you go to the game with your friends, you dress the same, order the same refreshments, and do the WAVE together.

When you go cycling with your club you wear the same Lycra shorts and jerseys, ride the same road bikes, and display the same excitement for the great outdoors. (And the Hell's Angels think they're all doing their "own thing" riding their Harleys, hiding behind their BOSS glasses, and flexing their blue body art punctuated by their nose rings.)

We mirror people every day whether we intend to or not. But once you become aware of it and how to use it, you can help more people solve more problems and feel better about themselves.

**Here's Looking
at You Kid**

36

Queen to Knight's f3

Are You Crazy?

After you've completed the following exercise shown to me by a couple of psychologists, try it on your friends.

Write down your first response to these five questions as quickly as you can without thinking. Each answer should take no more than two seconds. Ready? Here we go.

1. Name a color. _____
2. Name an animal in the zoo. _____
3. Name a piece of furniture. _____
4. Pick a number between 1 and 4. _____
5. Name a flower. _____

Pens down.

Doing this exercise at our seminars, I read my answers and have our attendees stand up if they have the same ones. It's never failed – the overwhelming majority always has at least two or more of the same answers. And the further down you go on the list, the more people stand up.

The answers:

1. The color? Red.
2. An animal in the zoo? Lion.
3. A piece of furniture? Chair.
4. The number between 1 and 4? 3.
5. The flower? A rose.

The value of this lesson? As the psychologists taught me, most people will respond predictably, while those with *emotional conflicts* might make uncommon associations. This is good to know when selling because now you'll know how to develop the right questions to ask that will get the predictable answers you're looking for.

After all, when you're cold calling, wouldn't you like to know who's hiding behind Door #1, Door #2, or Door #3 before you pick up that telephone? Is it a raging lion behind Door #1? A charging rhino behind Door #2? Or the most dangerous predator of all – the politician – behind Door #3? Once you know, you'll be prepared.

In chapter 25, "The Best Question to Ask on a First Sales Call", you saw that when you ask "Is now a good time?" you will get four predictable responses every time. Knowing this, you'll be 2-3 steps ahead of your prospect and positioned for your next move.

In chapter 12, "Would You Like Me to Wash That Brain for You?", you saw how to develop your seven qualifying questions using this knowledge of predictability. Knowing how to ask the right questions at the right time is like playing chess, predicting your opponent, and setting up your strategy six or seven moves in advance.

By the way, in a group of 300-400 people, maybe ten won't get any of the five. I tell them I won't point them out to the rest of the audience and embarrass them, but they may want to call the Betty Ford Center. Operators are standing by.

Don't let me stop you if you have a call to make.

37

It's Not Magic

If You Know How It's Done

I have my **Magic 6** questions I want to get answers to as early as I can in the selling process. Knowing the answers to these questions will help me better prepare for the interview and meet my prospects at their level.

Three salespeople from the same company attended one of our seminars and asked me afterwards if I would talk with their owner about doing some further training with their group. I said I had six questions I'd like to ask. Would they mind?

Not at all.

"First question. Is your boss direct or indirect in dealing with others?"

They all said he's very direct.

"Is he open or closed with his emotions?"

Closed.

"Describe his background. Entrepreneurial? Technical? Sales oriented?"

Without hesitating: entrepreneurial.

"Describe his dress. Is he conservative? Casual? Flamboyant?"

Conservative.

"Tell me about his office. In particular, what's on his desk at the end of the day?"

They thought about it and laughed.

"On his wall to the left," the man said, "just as soon as you walk into his office, you'll see a picture of his prized possession. His 70′ sailboat he loves like a child."

"His desk," the other man added, "is cleaned off at the end of the day. Not a scrap of paper to be found. And it's the largest desk in the office."

"Finally," I asked, "what adjectives would you use to describe your boss?"

"Well," the lady said, "he's very direct in dealing with you and wants to get to the bottom line immediately. Rather impatient. Sarcastic humor. He's quick to judge others. Some people read him as being a little harsh, but he's a great leader and we'd follow him to the ends of the earth."

Cheesehead

The greatest escape I ever made was when I left Appleton, Wisconsin.

- Houdini

Taking this information, do you think their boss is an Analytical, Driver, Expressive, or Amiable personality?

Driver all the way. Great information to have before making that first contact.

Later the following week I called and got an appointment with their boss. He said to be there by 1:30 p.m. Thursday. I could have fifteen minutes of his time. A definite sign of a Driver.

When I got to the appointment fifteen minutes early, I played like Sherlock Holmes and started gathering clues. Exactly at 1:30 I was shown into his office. Another sign of a Driver. They're prompt. We shook hands. He gave me the Driver's handshake (we will discuss that in a later chapter). Another clue I'm looking for. Looking to my left, I saw the photo of his sailboat I was told would be hanging on the wall.

To break the ice, to do a little bonding, should we talk about his salt sea baby? You better know the answer to this.

No way! Drivers could care less about bonding and small talk. If they do business with you later, maybe they'll have lunch with you or take you sailing. Besides, I was told I would have fifteen minutes and the clock was ticking.

I'd done my homework. I had discovered his company's sales goals for the coming year. Knowing that Drivers don't like to trade questions back and forth – they'd rather do all the talking while you do all the listening – I better speak first.

"So tell me," I asked as I was taking my seat, "what are your sales goals for the coming year?"

His eyebrows flashed and his eyes got as big as silver dollars. "You really want to know?" he asked excitedly.

You bet.

Now he surprised me. He turned around to his credenza, took out twenty-five loose-leaf notebooks and spread them across the top of his desk. Twenty-five salespeople's business plans for how they planned to meet their sales goals for the coming year. And then he started going over them in detail.

I glanced at my watch. We're still on book one, chapter one, paragraph one and my fifteen minutes are up. I wanted to honor my promise of time.

"Excuse me," I said, "but my fifteen minutes are up. Should we continue on, or should I come back at a later date?"

I thought he was going to jump out of his chair. He was so animated; he started waving his arms and shaking his head.

"No, no, no, Jerry! *You* are the most interesting person I have ever talked with. Let me show you more!"

He was the most interesting person I had ever talked with. I just knew the right question to ask and to shut up.

I barely talked for the next hour and fifteen minutes. A few well placed questions kept him going. Drivers like to talk and direct. Drivers want to be in control. They appreciate a good audience. I knew this and planned accordingly.

I also knew that Drivers can make a decision on the first one or two calls. I was sure I could get a vote up or down on this one. Knowing this before walking in made the conclusion anti-climatic. I walked out of his office with the signed contract. But I wouldn't have been able to pull it off if I didn't know what I was looking for.

It's not magic if you know how it's done.

38

Six Hours?

Man, I Could Have Done This in 20 Minutes!

Many behaviors are predictable, allowing you to determine the type of personality you're selling to. Why is this important?

1. You know how to open and conduct the call.
2. You can anticipate the responses and reactions you'll get.
3. You can modify and adjust your behavior to create faster rapport.
4. You know how many calls it will take to close the sale.
5. You know whether to ask questions or to listen.
6. You know whether to present a lot of facts – or sell with enthusiasm.

Look again at our personality matrix. (For excellent information on personalities, read Tony Alessandra's *The Platinum Rule: Discover the Four Basic Business Personalities and How They*

Can Lead You to Success, Jo-Ellan Dimitrius' *Reading People: How to Understand People and Predict Their Behavior – Anytime, Anyplace*, and David Peoples' *Selling to the Top: David Peoples' Executive Selling Skills*.)

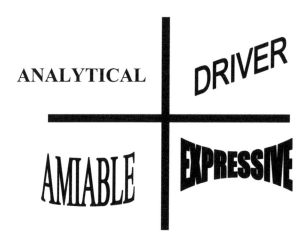

Remember that 15% of the people you call on are Drivers and can make a decision on the first one or two calls. 15% are Expressives who can make a decision in two to three calls. 35% are Amiables who make decisions within four to five calls. And 35% are Analyticals who take five to seven calls before they'll advance to the next stage of the selling process.

Spotting Drivers at our seminars is easy. Especially if they've been there for the entire six hour program. They're antsy. They're squirming in their seats. They take few notes. They roll their eyes.

I tell the audience, "My sympathies go out to the Drivers here today – because this seminar is *killing* you! You're thinking to yourself, 'Man – this is a six hour seminar? I could have done this in 20 minutes! What's taking so long? Just give me the facts. I'll fill in the details later.'"

About 15% of the audience starts doing their seminar bobble-head impressions.

"But," I continue, "the Analyticals are doing exactly the opposite. You're saying to yourself, 'Whoa! Slow down. Where's the fire? You're going too fast. This is a six hour seminar? This should be a six day seminar! I need more details.'"

I think I'm getting seasick as I see the waves of nodding heads increase to half the audience.

"And the Amiables? Well, you're thinking, 'Where's all the touchy-feely stuff? Why don't we have more role plays? Why don't we have a group hug?'"

Now they're scaring me.

Finally, the Expressives. "You're thinking, 'Where's all the glamour? The glitz? The strobe lights? The laser lights? The rockin' music? Why aren't you jumping up and down on the stage?'"

The point? You can't please all the people all the time. When you're selling you have to throw in something for all the different personalities so they can relate to you.

Test your knowledge

Where would these people fall in the personality matrix?

"Gil Grissom" the head honcho on TV's CSI? Analytical. Of course. He has to know every itsy-bitsy detail. This guy studies the tiniest of bugs crawling through your orifices. You'd expect a real CSI type to be the Analytical. The same is true for doctors, attorneys, and CPAs.

How about President George W. Bush or Simon Cowell of *American Idol* fame? Drivers. No doubt about it. They don't care about other people's opinions. They're direct. "Did I hurt your feelings? Aww, too bad." Drivers are judgmental and make quick decisions. They are, after all, the Deciders.

Let's Moo-o-o-ve Along
Why are you having a normal conversation with him? This is a dairy farmer dressed as a woman.
- Simon Cowell

What about Kelly Ripa (*Live with Regis & Kelly*) or Ann Curry (*Today Show*)? Amiables. They're emotional, touchy-feely, and are comfortable with small "sweet" talk. They're the mavens of group hug.

What about football legend (in his mind) and perennial All-Pro Terrell Owens? Expressive all the way. It's all about "ME ME ME!" Flashy. Wants all the limelight. Fast cars, fast times. Every sentence is flowered with "I I I I I".

Which is your personality? Now ask your friends if they agree. Surprised?

Chameleons

But what if you can't tell the personality of the person you're dealing with? What's going on? For example, you and three co-workers meet an interesting lady at a seminar. As you're driving back to the office, you're trying to peg her style.

The driver of the car thinks she's an Analytical. The front seat passenger disagrees. "No. Definitely an Expressive."

"What are you talking about?" the back seat passenger asks. "She's an Amiable if she's anything."

"Are you crazy," you shout, "she's a Driver all the way."

What happened? Your mutual friend had the ability to mirror each one of you instantly. She's a chameleon. She reflected back each person's distinctive personality. The driver of the car is himself an Analytical. The front passenger is an Expressive. The rear seat passenger is an Amiable. And you're the Driver. Each one of you liked her because she looked, acted and sounded just like you. It's a compliment that someone can mirror and quickly take on the identity of each person they meet. People in leadership positions will go far if they can master this skill.

Three of the four personalities are good at mirroring. Only one has trouble. The Driver. Drivers aren't concerned about pleasing others. They don't stoop to someone else's level. You have to meet them at theirs.

Here's a laundry list of things to look for when dealing with others.

Drivers

Reserved and unemotional. They're direct, assertive, aggressive, and forward in talking with you. Their motto: be direct, be brief, be gone. Like Analyticals, don't try to sell them with enthusiasm – they're not buying it.

They're entrepreneurs, often in upper management, and have a degree in business or economics. Drivers are conservative in their dress. They have the larger desks, usually cleared off at the end of the day, awards on their walls, and sit in high back chairs.

"I'm the Decider"
In my sentences I go where no man has gone before.

- George W. Bush

Adjectives to describe them: they need little information to make quick decisions, want the big picture with no details, have poor time management, impatient, quick tempers, sarcastic humor, judgmental, and not into relationships. They think they can be in two places at once, don't want input from others, dominate the talking, love to boss, are pushy, and don't understand why others can't get on with their lives like they can.

They don't like to answer questions, but they love to tell you things. They expect you to listen. Got a problem? Take a minute...now get over it. They don't embarrass easily, not afraid to ask for what they want, not affected by rejection, and empathy is foreign to them. When they ask you for the time, don't tell them how to build the watch.

Drivers go with their gut feelings and can't and won't adapt to others. They could be great cold callers because they don't get their feelings hurt and they're not sensitive if they hurt the feelings of others. But they're not good cold callers because they don't like small talk, relationship building, selling, and the details it takes to be successful at it. Their motto: "It's my way or the _____." Their arch enemy? The Amiables. "Man, will you ever stop crying?"

Analyticals

Like Drivers, they don't show their emotion; conservative in their dress. They're indirect in dealing with you, reclusive, and would enjoy being hermits. Unlike Drivers, they're not confrontational. Their thought for the day? "I'll think about it. Call me back next week."

They often have degrees in engineering, accounting, or computer sciences. Doctors, attorneys, and CPAs dominate the field.

They're deep thinkers, very detailed in their work, and are often authors.

In their office, you'll see diplomas on their walls and symbols of achievement. They want to prove to you they are who they say they are. If you walk into a client's office and see those diplomas, don't give them all the information on the first sales call as this is going to be a *very* long selling cycle.

Drivers cannot sell to them; they don't have the patience. Analyticals appear to be indecisive, but they're not. They only want to be sure before moving forward. They need all the details. Their desks are functional with every drawer in neat order and if they have papers on their desk at the end of the day, they're stacked in neat piles.

Adjectives: they have a dry sense of humor, more formal, precise, and not casual in their speech, hold others accountable, can never get enough information, analyze everything to death, love to talk strategies and tactics, see others' points of view and can easily adapt to other people's ways of thinking. They love to trade questions back and forth. But just the facts, ma'am.

When the Analytical asks you for the time, he's really asking, "How do you build that watch?" They're good with time management and don't want wasted motions. They are impatient, want to see proof of what you're saying, and will hold it against you if you're proven wrong. They want to be in control and have a hard time dealing with ambiguities. Unlike drivers, they don't trust themselves or listen to their intuitions.

The Drivers and Analyticals make up the majority of Fortune 500 top-level decision-makers. The personality that drives them crazy? The Expressives. Damned show-offs! They see Expressives as good at starting projects, but poor in their follow-up.

Amiables

These are the den mothers of the personalities. "Would you like cookies with that milk?" Like Analyticals, they're indirect in dealing with you and because they're emotional, their feelings are easily hurt. If they graduated from college, they probably have a degree in liberal arts.

They're good volunteers and are comfortable with public contact. Their dress is casual and tasteful. In their office you'll find pictures of family (faced in towards them and away from their guests), mementos, and their office is comfortable and home-like. Amiables have green things growing in their office that should be growing in there. Don't confuse them with the Expressives who have green things growing in their offices that have no business being in there.

Adjectives: easy going, want to please others, want to be liked and won't do things to upset others. Friendly, open, honest, believe in others, thoughtful, caring, and sincere when they laugh. However, this is the only group that has trouble making decisions on their own. If you're dealing with the Amiable, find who he or she is going to for advice and get them involved in every step of the selling process. Rarely will you see an Amiable person rise to a top-level decision-maker's position in a Fortune 500 company.

Amiables like small talk at the beginning of your first meeting because they have to feel they can trust you before they'll buy from you. And if you can talk about family, even better. The personality that would get them steamed (if they dared to show it): Drivers. They see them as being too harsh and mean; too domineering; non-listeners. And they're right. But as Drivers say, "So what!"

Expressives

Emotional and outgoing. Like Drivers, they're aggressive, forward and very direct in dealing with you. Many are in the field of sales, although they don't necessarily make the best salespeople. They are joiners and socializers. Their favorite sentence is, "Let's talk about me."

They're the peacocks of dress – flamboyant and bright colors. They'll wear large colorful hats to draw your attention to their beautiful face. They want to be noticed. You can't say enough good things about them. If you run out, they'll give you a list of things you forgot to mention. You can never thank them or compliment them enough. Their office is full of awards, accolades, and trophies.

So...the only question left is...?
I'm not offended by dumb blonde jokes because I know I'm not dumb. I also know I'm not blonde.
- Dolly Parton

And check out the pictures on their desk. They're usually turned out facing towards you the guest. Look closely and see who you recognize in the photographs. You'll see the Expressive standing or sitting with a celebrity of some type: politician, athlete, or Hollywood star. They're showing off. They want to impress you. Let them know you're impressed. They want you to not only see but to comment about their connections.

They have a messy desk at the end of the day. They know there's a desk under all those papers somewhere because they know that papers can't levitate. They need to be sold with lots of enthusiasm and hype.

Adjectives: they always speak in the first person (I, me). They're boisterous, braggadocio, and have high energy. "No" is not an answer. They're loud, want to be the center of attention, and laugh loudly. They're poor listeners (since you're not talking about them), self-absorbed, talk fast, have good ideas, but fail to follow-through. They love to talk about two sports: football and baseball. Don't know why. Analyticals can't stand them. ("Will you ever shut up?") In return, Analyticals drive them nuts. "Man, can't you make up your mind? You're driving me crazy."

Doing our seminar in Detroit, two men sitting on the front row kept laughing and nudging each other as I explained the personalities. After the program they introduced themselves. Life-long friends.

"Jerry, we wish we would have met you when we married our first wives. (They were divorced and re-married now.) I'm very much the Driver and my wife was the Amiable. My friend Charley here is the Analytical and his wife was the Expressive. Now we understand why we lost our houses."

If we could have known then what we know now. Now you know.

39

Sleight of Hand

The Most Important Contact

Whether you're doing walk-in cold calls, networking, or meeting customers for the first time, the most important two seconds will be when you shake hands. Judgments will be made in the blink of an eye. Business and jobs can be won or lost when hands meet.

You Can Do More
The more you do, the more you learn.
- Unknown

At a Houston seminar I needed an audience member to be my partner on the stage as I demonstrated the various handshakes. A senior executive from an oil company I met before the program volunteered. As he came to the stage, and as the rest of the audience was pairing up with their partners, he said something to me. I asked if he'd share that information with the rest of the audience.

He said his company had been interviewing for a sales position and had narrowed the selection down to one young man. He had every qualification they needed. He was well educated, had a good track record, and had an excellent personality. They thought he had the "goods" to succeed in their business.

The senior executive said that last week he had been sitting in the chairman's office, along with the president of the company, waiting for the man to come in for the final interview; the interview where they would offer him the job.

My partner on the stage said, "Out of the blue the chairman turned to me and said, 'Did you notice how the man shakes hands?'"

Surprised, the senior executive said, "Yes. But I thought he just did that with me."

"No," the chairman said as he shook his head, "he did it with me and he did it with the president. And now I find out he did it with you. You better tell him that if he wants this job, he better *never* shake hands like that again."

The senior executive got the message. He excused himself and went downstairs to intercept the man before his appointment with the chairman.

Taking the applicant to his office, the senior executive said, "The job is yours. The contract is on the chairman's desk. Guaranteed six figure income. But we have one problem."

The man was excited. What's the problem?

"The chairman told me that you used the same handshake with him and the president that you used with me. He said he doesn't like that. He said you better never use that handshake again. He said that if you use that handshake with our customers and prospects you'll alienate them. So you can't do it again. Ever."

The man was confused. He didn't understand what they were talking about. The executive explained. The man nodded his head. Understood.

The senior executive and future salesman continued with some chit-chat until the chairman was ready for the signing. The man was nervous and excited. He got up to take leave of the senior executive, shook his hand, and told him how much he appreciated the opportunity to work at his company.

But guess how he shook hands? That's right. Exactly the same way.

After the senior executive released the man's hand, he said, "Son, the job is no longer yours. You're going to have to start looking somewhere else."

"Wait a minute," I asked my partner, "do you mean you didn't hire a highly qualified man simply because of his handshake?"

"No," replied the executive, "that was the second strike against him."

Second?

"That's right. His first strike? He didn't listen. I told him *exactly* what it would take to get this job and he didn't listen to me. At this company, with our chairman, and with what I was told, if I would have sent him in there and he used that handshake again, I would have been called onto the carpet. At our company, two strikes and you're out."

A small thing. A tiny thing. A simple handshake.

I've had many people use that same handshake on me. Would you like to know what that handshake was so you won't repeat it? I thought you would. But...like Paul Harvey says...that will be the "rest of the story" in a later chapter.

Avoiding political suicide

Handshakes are important not only in business, but in politics. In a *60 Minutes* interview President Bill Clinton related that in September 1993, when he brought Israel's Prime Minister Yitzhak Rabin and Palestinian Chairman Yassar Arafat together on the south lawn of the White House to sign their peace accords, he was faced with a dilemma.

Who's for Lunch?
The one sure way to conciliate a tiger is to allow oneself to be devoured.

- Konrad Adenauer

Before going outside for the ceremonies, Prime Minister Rabin pulled President Clinton aside and said he would shake hands with Chairman Arafat, but that he would not, under any circumstances, participate in the Arab custom of kissing on the cheeks. He said that would be the "kiss of death" for such a picture to live on in history.

Not knowing what to do, President Clinton got with his aide Tony Lake. They had to devise a plan to stop Arafat from embracing Rabin. Lake came up with an ingenious plan.

Lake said that Clinton must first shake hands with Arafat before shaking hands with Rabin. As they were shaking hands, Clinton was to take his left hand and put it on the inside of Arafat's upper right arm – his biceps. If Arafat tried to move in on Clinton with the traditional kiss on the cheeks, Clinton was to stiffen his left arm and force Arafat to keep his distance. Then, since Arafat couldn't kiss Clinton, he would not be allowed to kiss Rabin as it would not be proper to kiss one and not the other.

Sure enough, as Clinton was shaking hands with Arafat, Arafat tried to move in. Clinton kept him at a distance. Releasing hands, Arafat then shook hands with Rabin. No kissing. The now famous picture of the two shaking hands with Bill Clinton between them shows two men, stiff-armed, unwilling to leave their "territory" while keeping the other at a safe distance.

Unity now!?*

In North America there are four basic zones of comfort people have when interacting with others. One of those zones, the intimate zone, is 6" – 18" from the chest. Only people who are emotionally close to the other person are permitted to enter that zone.

Extend your right arm straight out. Measure the distance from your chest to the palm of your hand. 18". When someone extends his hand to you, you're invading his personal zone reserved for very few. Don't abuse the trust. And gauge his handshake to measure how you're affecting his emotions and thoughts. They are revealed in the grasp and strength of his handshake.

Are handshakes important? How do you think this dinner went? On September 28, 2006, President George W. Bush hosted a dinner in his private residence at the White House for two of America's allies in the fight on terrorism, Afghan President Hamid Karzai and Pakistani President General Pervez Musharraf. Allies who could barely look each other in the eye.

According to the AP report, "In a Rose Garden appearance arranged to show warmth and unity, the bickering leaders of Pakistan and Afghanistan shook hands with President Bush but not with each other."

Warmth? Unity? What was Karzai's and Musharraf's message to each other? To President Bush? To the world? To the terrorists? Are handshakes important? Can they be read? Does anyone notice?

Let's take a look at some of the most common handshakes you'll experience.

40

Palm Down

Put-Down Artist

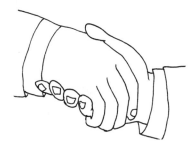 *The information on handshakes is based upon years of research as well as interviews and training at our national Cold Calling for Cowards® seminars with thousands of participants. These handshake examples apply only in the American culture and are not gender specific. An excellent resource for handshakes and body language can be found in Allan & Barbara Pease's* The Definitive Book of Body Language.

Ever wonder if you're meeting a top-level decision-maker? Their handshake may give them away.

If the person you're meeting shakes your hand with his or her palm angled more towards the ground, you've met such a person. Allan Pease found that 78% of upper-management people shake hands by forcing the palm of your hand up in a submissive manner. Plus, they're more likely to be the ones to initiate the handshake.

The message? "I want to be in control. I want to give the orders. I want you to obey. I want you to listen to me." What should you do? Ask few questions, listen, and don't interrupt. Be direct. Be brief. Be gone. But don't be fooled.

Two countertactics

What is your countertactic so you both can still get what you want without you being submissive? You have two choices. I like the first one best. Simply ignore the put-down. As General George Patton observed, "A tactic perceived is no longer a tactic." I know you're trying to get the upper-hand, it's not going to work, game over.

The second tactic involves a barely perceptible twist of the wrist. Rarely will the dominant greeter be able to discern what you did on a conscious level, but he will pick it up on a subconscious level.

If someone greets you with his palm down, step into him with your *left* foot, relax your right arm (because it instantly relaxes his arm) but don't let go of his hand; then twist your wrist to the left until the edges of both hands are parallel to the ground. The message sent and received: "You won't dominate me, and I won't try to dominate you. We're equals."

And here's a bonus to this technique. When you step into your partner with your left foot, notice if he holds his ground or if he takes a step back. If he holds his ground, you know this is going to be a tough negotiation because he won't back down. However, if he takes a step back, he feels intimidated because you invaded his space, and now you've gained the upper-hand.

In addition to top-level decision-makers using this handshake, most all Driver personalities use it to intimidate others. That's why I love to see two Drivers meeting each other.

It's not a trick, it's a fact

Please don't write to me saying I'm being tricky or devious or trying to teach you how to be. I'm not and I wouldn't. I'm simply the messenger.

Doing sales training with a large daily newspaper, one of my students told me their group had recently completed negotiations with management for a new contract. None of my attendees were aware of it, until I brought it up, that all 15 of their managers had used the palm down handshake on them during the negotiations. I asked for the names of some of the managers because I wanted to interview them.

"Why did you use the palm down handshake?" I asked the managers.

They grinned sheepishly. "We went to a seminar on how to shake hands and were taught to use that specific handshake if we wanted to improve our odds for getting our terms in the contract. And guess what? It worked!"

Take the Wheel
People are more easily led than driven.
- David Fink

If the employees had known how to read that put-down, do you think things might have turned out differently?

Crying in his Milwaukee brew

During one of our Milwaukee seminars, one of the men embarrassingly volunteered some advice for the audience so they wouldn't repeat his mistake.

Several weeks earlier he had gone out to meet the CEO of her company and three of her vice presidents on his first sales call. He shook hands with the CEO first and then each of the men.

Immediately after he shook hands with the last man, she said to him, "Why did you shake hands with the men like you did, but yet shook my hand like you did?"

"What do you mean?" he asked.

"Well, I noticed that when you shook hands with the men, your palm was up. When you shook hands with me, your palm was down. I felt you were putting me down – and I don't like it!"

He said he wasn't even aware he had used two different handshakes. He also said now he understands why he never got invited back into that account and why the CEO never returns his calls.

This could give car salesmen a bad rap

Several car salesmen attended one of our Seattle seminars and thoroughly enjoyed the handshake exercise. They later shared a tactic with me I've never seen, would never use, and was shocked that their customers never became aware of it.

They said that when a prospect entered the showroom, they'd walk over and extend their hand in the palm up position. Then, with no subtlety at all, they quickly flipped the prospect's hand over until the salesman had the dominant palm down position. They designed the flip to be overt and obvious so the prospect would both see it and feel it.

"What do the prospects do? Leave?" I asked. I certainly would.

"Oh no. Not at all. And get this," one of the salesmen continued, "when the prospect is in the business manager's office preparing to sign the contract and financial papers for the new car, I'll wait until he gets seated, walk in, remain standing so I can further dominate him, and use the flip handshake again."

You're kidding. Right?

"No. The customer can *see* what's happening, but he doesn't *know* what's happening."

What is happening?

"We're taking control of the situation. We're going to dominate. We're making the customer submissive so he'll follow our directions. And he doesn't even know it."

Caveat emptor.

Are handshakes important?

Tip the messenger on your way out.

41

Palm Up

Put Them at Ease, Get Their Trust

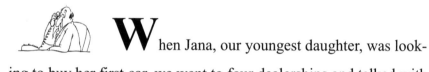**W**hen Jana, our youngest daughter, was looking to buy her first car, we went to four dealerships and talked with four salesmen. After driving away from the last dealer, I asked which salesman she liked best. (I had written down #3 on a piece of paper without showing her.) "I liked #3," she said. I showed her my note and she laughed.

I asked her why she picked him. "I dunno. I just seemed to like him better."

"Did you notice how he shook your hand?"

She shook her head. "No. Didn't pay any attention."

Of the four salesmen, he was the only one who greeted her with the palm *up* handshake. The other three salesmen greeted her by using their palm down handshake.

Compared to what was said about the palm down handshake, does this mean the palm up handshake is bad and leaves you in a submissive position? No. If you're the one to initiate the hand-

218

shake with the palm up you've actually gained the upper-hand. Like the third car salesman.

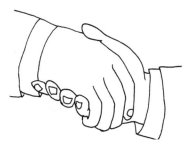

By initiating the palm up handshake you're telling the other party, "Welcome. Go ahead. You have the floor. I want to listen to what you have to say." The other person instantly relaxes, feels in control (because he's getting to use the palm down handshake), and he will be more open, honest, and candid with you.

Go ahead. Find two different people in your office. Walk over and shake hands with the first person, put your palm down and see how you feel. Then go over to a second person, extend your hand with your palm up and notice how you feel. Different, huh? Ask each person how they felt: dominant or submissive?

So which handshake will you use when greeting your customers or networking with friends? Which will you use when you try to get that long deserved raise from your boss? Which will he use to break the news you're not getting it?

42

The Dreaded Dead Fish

That Stinks!

Slip sliming away. Slip sliming away. The nearer your destination, the more you're slip sliming away.

My apologies to Paul Simon.

"When I'm interviewing for a sales position, if the candidate gives me the dead fish handshake, I eliminate him or her immediately." This from a woman sales manager who attended our seminar in Santa Clara.

"That quickly?" I asked.

"Just like that," she said snapping her fingers.

Before the candidate can say a word, he's gone in the sales manager's mind. Less than one-tenth of a second. Doesn't matter about his résumé, education or successes. He's outta' here.

Too bad for both the sales manager and the candidate.

Doesn't it bother you when someone gives you that dead fish? You just want to run your hands along your pants to make sure none of those slimy scales stuck. They say that your handshake is a reflection of your energy. The dead fish feels like it's ready to be gutted.

Most people who give you the dead fish don't even know it until you tell them. When you point out the limpness they're speechless, their jaw drops, and their face turns red.

But the dead fish handshake is the most misunderstood handshake there is. Most of us read it as the person is a wimp, weak, and not a decision-maker. No energy. Someone who can be bowled over.

Sure About That?
Confidence is contagious. So is lack of confidence.
- Vince Lombardi

But don't be so quick to judge. If someone gives me the dead fish, the first thing I want to know is, "What do you do for a living?" Or, "What kinds of hobbies do you have?"

Chances are, they work with their hands for a living or use their hands in their hobbies. Doctors, dentists, musicians, and artists depend on their hands. Service technicians have soft handshakes. They'd prefer not to shake to begin with. If they do, they want to get their hand in and out as quickly as possible so you won't weld their fingers together and ruin their livelihood.

Doing a seminar in the nation's capital, one of our attendees said he met golfing great Chi Chi Rodriguez. "He had the deadest fish handshake I've ever seen," the attendee said. But look what he does for a living. His hands are his tools.

What's the lesson? I told the sales manager not to be so quick to rule out sales candidates based solely upon the dead fish. Don't close your mind. Do some more investigating. Ask what kinds of hobbies they have. Told her she could be eliminating many qualified candidates simply because she didn't understand the message.

Also, people may have physical limitations. An attendee in Tucson said she had cerebral palsy and couldn't give a firm handshake. A lady in our St. Louis seminar said she has severe arthritis and if someone squeezes her hand, it takes days to recover.

But the rule of thumb in business (because so many people misread the dead fish) is to give a good, firm, web-to-web handshake.

Your job – your next sale – may depend on it.

43

Politician

Show Me the Money!

 **T**he double-handed politician's handshake has a double meaning. It depends upon who's giving and who's receiving.

The person who's initiating the handshake, that is the person using the double handshake on you, is trying to convey a feeling of sincerity and warmth. "Trust me. Believe me. I'm your best friend."

The problem is, the people on the receiving end receive the opposite message. They immediately become suspicious.

"Okay. What do you want? What are you up to? What's this about? I better watch my wallet."

That's why I also call it the "show me the money" handshake. (Saying it's the "politician's" handshake is repeating myself.)

Write Your Congressman
I once sent a dozen of my friends a telegram saying FLEE AT ONCE—ALL IS DISCOVERED. They left town immediately.

- Mark Twain

But there are exceptions to every rule. Ministers, priests, and rabbis will use the double handshake and people are comfortable with that level of intimacy. Healthcare professionals (doctors, nurses, caregivers, pre-need burial salespeople) tell me they've been taught to use this handshake to convey empathy and understanding. Not only is the handshake expected, but it is well received.

Be alert. This is one of the handshakes that will change quickly when meeting someone for the first time. When you meet the client notice how he or she shakes hands. In most business situations, it's the "we're equals" business shake with the edges of the hands parallel to the floor and with your hands touching web-to-web.

When you leave the meeting see if the client changes to a double handshake. If so, it's because she's become comfortable with you and trusts you. A good sign; you've gained points. You don't need to reciprocate with the double shake, but notice to see if it was given. Don't do anything to betray the trust you've started building.

Lesson learned: when meeting someone, especially for the first time, don't use the double handshake if you don't want her to feel uncomfortable and cautious. And if she uses it on you, don't vote for her.

44

The Traveling Arm

Don't Touch Me! Don't! Don't Do It!

What's the stereotypical picture you get of a used car salesman greeting his next victim, er, prospect on the lot? That's right. As he shakes his prey's hand, his left arm wraps around the shoulder of the buyer like they're old college room-mates. His shoulder lock warns you what he's really thinking, "You're not getting away from me this time, buddy."

How do you feel meeting a stranger for the first time when he shakes hands and draws you in like this? Uncomfortable? Feel like your space is being invaded?

What if it's your favorite uncle you haven't seen for years? It's okay? What if something tragic has just happened and a stranger uses this approach? Don't you feel comforted?

Allan Pease (*The Definitive Book of Body Language*) found that when people shake hands they express their emotions with the placement of their left hand on your right arm or shoulder. The higher up the left hand goes – from the double-clasp handshake, to your forearm, to your upper arm, to your shoulder – the stronger the feelings this person has for you.

In a business situation don't use your left hand to touch the other party. Otherwise you'll leave the impression that you're trying to move some inventory. (Pease found that if you lightly and quickly touch someone's right elbow as you're shaking hands, it can triple your chances of getting what you want.)

Once you get to know the other person on a personal level, touching with the left hand is more acceptable. But rarely is it acceptable to touch someone on his upper arm or shoulder unless he's a relative or unless something emotional has just happened between you.

That's why I like to watch entertainers like David Letterman or Jay Leno or Jon Stewart to see how they shake hands with their guests. If you watch their left hand, it gives an indication of how well they know their guests and how comfortable they are with them.

It's especially fun to watch Leno when his male guests come from behind the curtains to greet him. Leno is a hugger and tries to put his left hand on the guest's shoulder and do a shoulder-to-shoulder bump. But many of his guests approach him with their right arm stiffened to keep him at a distance. They either don't know him well enough for the hug, don't feel it's a sincere emotion from the host, or they're uncomfortable with any type of close contact in public.

Just a left-handed word of caution for the next time you meet the person you hope signs your contract.

45

The Half-Hand

Back Off!

**W**hen you reach to shake someone's hand and you grasp only her fingertips, how do you feel? Like you want to make some adjustments and try that again? Like you've met the Queen of England and she's waiting for you to kiss her hand?

Who made the bad grab – you or the person you're meeting? Should you try and reposition your hand and try it again? Should you say something about it? Or should you act as if nothing's happened? And what's the message?

Meeting thousands of people attending our seminars, many people used this handshake with me. It usually happened in the morning before the program started as I was walking around the ballroom meeting our guests. Both men and women of all ages would use the half-hand handshake with me.

What does it mean? "I'm uncomfortable with you. I don't know you. Please keep your distance." These people are usually insecure.

As I'm walking around and welcoming our guests, most attendees don't know who I am. I'm a complete stranger introducing myself to everyone there. I make them nervous. Often, if they saw me getting near, they'd bury their heads in their morning papers or suddenly decide there was an important call they had to return.

Most participants I meet with this handshake do one thing others with different handshakes don't do. They rarely stand up to greet me and remain seated instead. They're trying to remain small and invisible.

Recognizing the half-hand meant they were uncomfortable with me, I'd take a step away from them upon releasing hands and place both my hands behind my back in the palm-in-palm gesture. Doing this, they were relieved, smiled, and we had a good conversation.

Don't draw the half-hander's attention to his grip as this will make him self-conscious and embarrass him. Instead, read it for what it is and respond appropriately. Besides, he doesn't even know he's doing it. And because I know I always use the web-to-web handshake, I know I'm not the cause of the half-hand.

What should you do if you're a half-hander? Change your handshake to the web-to-web business handshake because you want to make other people comfortable with you. If you're seated, and someone walks over to shake hands, stand up. If you let the other person remain standing over you, he's in a dominating position and will make you feel even more insecure.

One of my best customers, before he passed away, was the president and CEO of the largest mail order arts supply company in the world. I'd known him for over eight years. And I knew he used the half-hand handshake. He was a brilliant man, but not a people person. Every time I went to his office to visit him, I'd try to shoot my hand in for the web-to-web handshake to get a full grip. But he was faster than me. He always cut me off with the half-hand. I worried that maybe I was doing something that made him uncomfortable. But then I watched how he'd greet his own staff, customers, and people we networked with. He used the same handshake on them. Whew! It wasn't just me.

What should you do if someone uses the half-hand on you? Do exactly as I do. When you release hands, take a step back and place both hands behind your back. Show her you have no weapons.

The worst thing you can do is to step into them. You will physically affect them. Their heart begins to race, their breathing gets rapid, and they'll even start perspiring. They're not listening to a word you have to say. They're wondering, "When does the attack start?"

Exception to the rule: many politicians will purposely use the half-hand when working the crowds for two reasons. First, because they shake thousands of hands each week they can get bleeding blisters and crushed fingers from overzealous constituents; they need to protect their hands. Second, their security people tell them to use this handshake so no one can get a firm grip on them and pull them into the crowd while giving the security people a chance to intervene and break the lock.

A *long* extension of the half-hand-keep-your-distance handshake is the Farmer in the Dell handshake. My dad was the minister at a small Texas church in the country outside of Waco when I was in junior high and high school. It was always fun watching the farmers and ranchers greet each other. In rural areas, their idea of a handshake is to stand ten to fifteen feet apart and give a wave and a nod. Touching is not allowed. To get any closer could get you bulldogged and branded.

Did you hear the one about...?
Times change. The farmer's daughter now tells jokes about the traveling salesman.
> *- Carey Williams*

46

Bone-Crusher

Secret from the Florida Highway Patrol

Arriving for some sales training in Clearwater, Florida, I was greeted by the company's owner at the door. I noticed he had an unusual handshake but said nothing about it.

At the end of the day, the owner walked me to the car, we exchanged pleasantries, and he shook my hand the same way again. I was curious.

"Why do you shake hands that way?"

"Oh," he said, "you noticed?"

"Hard to miss it," I laughed.

The owner told me that he was retired from 25 years of service with the Florida Highway Patrol before becoming the entrepreneur of his business.

"I use the technique to stop anyone from using a bone-crusher handshake on me whether they try to intimidate me or try to hurt me," he said. "And it works every time."

He was right. I've used his handshake on numerous occasions and have taught it to our seminar audiences. Women who wear rings especially like the tactic as men sometimes shake their hands with too much pressure. Men like it because they know some of their friends or customers use the bone-crusher to try and intimidate them. And the nice thing about the technique is that it doesn't take any strength. It's all leverage.

What did the retired Florida Highway Patrol officer teach me? When you shake hands, extend the forefinger of your hand straight so it slides past the heel of the other person's hand and touches his wrist (like you're taking his pulse with your forefinger). This positions your hand in such a way that regardless how strong or big the other person is, he can't get a grip on your hand and squeeze it.

"You want to see something else I can do with that handshake?" the owner asked me.

I'm game. "Sure."

He applied pressure with his forefinger to my pulse and dropped me to my knees.

"That's another reason we use it," he said. "So in case you have any ideas about harming me I can catch you by surprise and with little pressure take you down."

And here's another way to stop a bone-crusher several M.D.'s have taught me. Because they work with their hands for a living, they can't afford to have anyone squeeze their fingers or knuckles.

When you shake hands, cup your hand like you're trying to hold water in it. Keep your fingers together and make a pocket with the palm of your hand and then shake. It's impossible for someone to get their hand over yours and squeeze it.

Give it a shake.

47

To Shake or Not to Shake

The Rest of the Story

What if you're doing walk-in cold calls and you're talking with the receptionist at the front desk? Should you walk over and shake his or her hand?

After interviewing gatekeepers across the country, they say they prefer not to shake anyone's hand coming into the office for two reasons. First, they're busy answering the phones. Second, most of them have young children at home. They know that shaking hands is a fast way of taking colds home to their loved ones.

A simple nod of the head and quick "Hello" will do, thank you.

The same applies if you're working a trade show booth and you meet someone standing nearby. Keep your distance. (Remember the 18" rule and invading someone's personal space.) Simply nod your head and say "Hi". If they want to meet you, they'll come closer. But keep your hands by your side so they'll know it's okay to offer their hand if they choose to do so. If you keep your hands behind your back, they may feel you want your space. Hands in the pocket mean you don't want to be involved in a conversation.

Treat me as an equal

Doing some training with a large Southern California newspaper, we did a role play. I made one of the women the CEO and the other woman the president of their company. A man was to be the salesman. Nothing was rehearsed, and no directions were given.

The salesman came into their office, stopped about three feet from the desk and introduced himself. Both women, without any direction, stood up and came from around their desks to exchange pleasantries. The salesman made a few appropriate remarks and the women then returned to their desks and sat down. After 10 minutes the presentation was complete and the salesman left. I thought he did an excellent job.

I asked the women, "Would you do business with this man?"

Without looking at each other, they both said an emphatic "No!" simultaneously. I was surprised.

"Why not?"

"Because he didn't come over and shake our hands."

What?

"Look," said the president, "if we were men, he would have walked over to shake hands with us. We feel that since we're women he was treating us with less respect. We want to be treated as equals. If a man walks over to shake hands with another man, he darn well better walk over and shake mine."

How about that? The man lost the sale despite giving a great presentation. He lost it in less than two seconds. He lost it with a handshake. Or rather, the absence of a handshake.

National response

As I continued doing our seminars across the country, I began asking the men and women in our audiences the question of whether or not they thought men should initiate handshakes with women in business today.

About half the men said they thought it was still proper to wait for women to initiate the handshake. But they were surprised that 90% of the women said it was completely proper for the man to initiate the handshake in business. Otherwise, like the two California women, they felt disrespected and not treated as equals.

Go On
The Half Fast Research company reports that 9 out of 10.

- Unknown

One caveat on men initiating handshakes: be sensitive to the part of the country you're in and the age of the women you're shaking hands with. In the deep South, more women tell me they still prefer to be the ones to initiate the handshake. And if the women are older, they too, prefer to be the ones to initiate the handshake.

How do you know it's safe to walk over and shake hands? Look for clues. If you're walking into the executive's office and she remains behind her desk (sitting or standing), the desk is serving as a shield of protection. I'd remain three or four feet away, out of arm's length, and give a nod and greeting. But if she gets up and comes from around her desk and "invades" my territory (like the California women), I'll take a step over and extend my hand because she has no fear and feels superior.

Something else women complain about with the way men shake their hands. They said to tell men that they're not fragile china dolls who will crack under a firm handshake. Many men tell me that they will deliberately give women the Half-Hand handshake or Dead Fish handshake because they don't want to "hurt their hands". The women hate this. "Give me a firm grip, just like you would another man."

Physically challenged

Doing a seminar in the nation's capital, I was working the room and meeting attendees before the program started. A man sitting on the end of the row remained seated when I walked over to introduce myself. I stuck out my right hand. He extended his left. His right arm was paralyzed. I quickly dropped my right hand, extended my left and exchanged greetings.

When we got to the handshake exercise of the seminar, I asked the man if I could get some advice from him for the audience. He knew what I was going to ask, smiled, and said, "Sure."

"I don't know the answer to this, so you'll have to educate me. When we met this morning you extended your left hand and I extended mine. Did I do the right thing?"

He turned to the audience and told those who weren't aware of it that he had lost the use of his right arm as a child. He could only shake with his left hand.

"You did the right thing, Jerry," he said. "If someone doesn't have the use of his right arm and he extends his left, it's best if you extend your left."

Then he got a chuckle out of the audience. "What I don't like, is if I extend my left hand and you still shake it with your right. Then I feel uneasy. Like we're partners walking down the beach."

A similar situation happened in another city. I met a man before the seminar got started and watched his interaction with other audience members before the program began. I was nervous about how he would respond to the handshaking exercise of the program. But he did great. He laughed, had fun, and got a kick out of it. Then he educated all 400 of us.

After the audience had been seated, I called on him and asked if he'd mind answering a question that had been bothering me. He knew where I was going with this.

"There are several hundred people here and they can't see you. Would you mind standing up so they can hear you?"

He did.

"Again, I don't know the answer to this, and I certainly don't want to embarrass you, but do you like for people to shake hands with you?"

The people in the back of the room couldn't see what I was getting at.

My friend in the audience held up both hands. He had none.

"I have 'hooks for hands'," he told the group. He had lost his hands in an accident.

"Yes," he continued, "I wish people would walk over and shake my hook. It's my hand. I'd like to be treated like a normal person. But sometimes the hooks intimidate people. I understand. And I won't hold it against you. But it's okay to treat me like a regular person."

I think I'm in love

What about the person you're shaking hands with and she won't let go? She keeps shaking and shaking and shaking.

I have only one question: when was your last date?

Watching the Amazing Kreskin (the famed mentalist) on Johnny Carson one night, I thought he was going to shake Johnny's arm out of its socket. He looked like he was pumping for oil. "Geez," Johnny said rubbing his shoulder, "you shake so hard. What the hell's the matter with you?"

Kreskin laughed. "Oh, I do that with everyone. I'm just so excited to see you!"

I Feel Good
They may forget what you said, but they will never forget how you made them feel.
- Carl W. Buechner

Other findings

Allan Pease found all countries have a certain number of pumps in their handshakes. He found that Americans have five to seven. However, based on the thousands of handshakes I've witnessed in our seminars, I notice about three to four wears out most Americans.

Asians prefer not to shake hands or touch. Bowing takes its place.

A man at our Anaheim seminar told me that he was the interpreter for General Norman Schwarzkopf during the first Gulf War. He said in the Middle East that the softer the handshake, the more of a Dead Fish it is, the more power that person wields. And remember that photo of President George W. Bush holding hands and strolling on his Texas ranch with Saudi Crown Prince Abdullah? Did the press catch them on a date? No. According to Pease, if a Saudi man is holding hands with another man in public it's a sign of mutual respect.

But even in America, handshakes are not true across the board. Doing a Phoenix seminar, some women from the Apache and Navajo nations were talking with me after the program. One of the ladies said that in their cultures they'd prefer not to touch each other to begin with. They said they were trying to get accustomed to "the white man's ways" of shaking hands, but if given a choice, they'd really rather not touch.

The rest of the story

Oh, and the rest of the story about that salesman who lost the job offer in Houston. Remember the guy who had a guaranteed six figure contract sitting on the chairman's desk waiting to be signed? And the chairman said he better never use that handshake again? What handshake did the salesman use that lost him the job?

The Palm Down handshake. The chairman said that he read that as a "put down" (true), that the salesman was a talker and not a listener (as he proved with the senior executive), and that the salesman would try to dominate his customers (true again).

And now you know…the rest of the story.

48

Which Part of the Anatomy Was That?

Things They Never Taught You in Biology

It's been said that people lie but body language doesn't. If you're in doubt whether to believe what you're being told, or to believe what you see, body language carries five times the weight of the spoken word.

Every Winter Olympics season the network brings out the old tapes of the Tonya Harding – Nancy Kerrigan knee capping escapade and I get a kick out of watching Tonya in her press conference denying she had anything to do with the incident.

After watching the original news conference, I told my wife I didn't believe her, she was doing something obvious to show she wasn't being truthful, but I couldn't put my finger on it. She was hiding behind the lectern, palms clinched shut, shoulders slumped, and chin down. Enough visual clues to draw a conclusion. But she was doing something I could see but couldn't comprehend. I watched a tape of the conference about twenty times that night. And then I caught it. I told my wife, "Watch her head."

As Tonya is standing behind the lectern denying her involvement, her head is down and she's commenting, "I had nothing to do…with the planned assault…on Nancy Kerrigan." As she was proclaiming her innocence her head was shaking in disagreement with her words.

Tonya went to Lillehammer, performed, and returned to face the charges. She pleaded guilty to conspiracy, but hey, all she did was pick the hammer and the knee. Otherwise, she was innocent.

If you're ever in doubt, trust your eyes. Body language is a true barometer of your attitudes and emotions, regardless of what your words declare.

Suppose, as you're speaking to a prospect, he rubs or holds the back of his neck. What's his message?

You can take it literally. You, or what you're saying, is a pain in the neck. (Make sure you understand which part of the anatomy he's grabbing though.)

What should you do? Keep in mind that the longer someone holds a physical position, he will hold the accompanying attitude with it – negative or positive. Since this is a negative gesture, you want to replace his negative attitude. And it's easier to change his body language than it is to change his mind.

Look at This
The person who can capture and hold attention is the person who can effectively influence human behavior.

- H.A. Overstreet

Hand the prospect your business card, a brochure, or something that he has to reach for with the offending hand. The instant he reaches, his attitude shifts. Then transition into another topic or subject that won't be so irritating.

There are several obvious body language clues that telegraph what people are thinking and what their answers will be before they say a word. If you're sensitive to them you may save the deal and perhaps avoid getting shown the door. With some exceptions, body language gestures are not gender specific, but they do differ between cultures. The ones discussed here apply only to the American culture.

Easy to notice gestures:
1. Hand-to-face
2. Shaking hands
3. Eye movements
4. Hand gestures
5. Arm gestures
6. Leg gestures

Are you a mentalist?

You're talking to the prospect. You make a benefit statement that is so good to be true that it should sell the product on its own. You notice the prospect scratches the side of her neck. Does she have an itch?

No. She doubts what you said. She has a silent objection.

If you want to scare her, stop your presentation and instead comment, "I see you have a question. Would you mind sharing your thoughts with me?"

She'll probably be startled and think, "Can this guy read my mind? What's going on?"

By observing body language clues, you'll be able to uncover objections they're afraid to voice. You'll then have the opportunity to discuss them and provide a remedy.

Let us pray

Next situation. You're sitting in the prospect's office. He's relaxed, leaning back in his chair, arms crossed. His chin is lowered slightly and he has a slight lip-tight smile, nodding his head as you speak.

As you finish your last statement, he leans forward, places both elbows on the desk, and raises his hands into a raised steeple position (the fingertips are lightly touching). It looks like his hands are in a prayer position.

Should you ask for the order? Or is he praying that you'll leave?

The raised steeple position is a sign of confidence. He's confident of one of two things. He's confident he's going to buy your product, or confident he's going to throw you out on the street. In this situation, which is it and why? What are the clues?

Any time you see someone take the raised steeple position, try to remember what he was doing immediately before he made this gesture and you'll have your answer.

Need a GPS?
Now that I'm here, where am I?

- Janis Joplin

First clue: he was leaning away from you and not into you. Not good. Like he was trying to keep as much distance between the two of you as possible. Second clue: his arms were crossed. Like he's blocking you with a shield for protection. He's defensive and not trusting. Third clue: his chin was down. When the chin is down, people are negative and judgmental. Forget his smile and nodding head. Chances are the smile was only a lip courtesy. The nod of the head was probably to placate you and hurry you on to the finish so he could get his turn.

In other words, "You're outta' here!"

What should you do? Don't ask for the order. He's confident he's going to get rid of you. Instead, change the subject, or introduce some rock solid evidence that will support what you're saying. Again, if you want to surprise him, say, "I get the feeling you don't completely agree with what I'm saying. Do you have some reservations, because I'm still not sure if we're the right fit for you at this time?"

By taking the wind out of his sails, he'll see that you're not trying to corner him into a decision and that you do want to help him find the right solution. Plus, you stop him from verbalizing "No" and creating commitment and consistency on himself. If you let him say no, he'll have to save face and stick with his decision to say it's a no-go.

Pinocchio effect

These next two tips saved a company in San Diego $2000 the sales manager told me. After the seminar, the sales manager and his salesman said they were going on a sales call the next day to visit a prospect they hadn't seen for a couple of months.

"We don't know if we're still in the running to be a vendor, and we don't know if they still have the money in the budget," the sales manager told me. "What should we look for?"

I told them. The following day, waiting in the airport to fly out to Phoenix, my office called. The sales manager in San Diego wanted me to call him.

When I called, the sales manager asked to put me on hold while he went to get the salesman. "Do you mind if I put you on the speakerphone?" he asked when he returned. Not at all.

"Jerry, we went to see the customer we told you about yesterday. We wanted to thank you. You saved us $2000." I could hear them laughing in the background.

"What happened?"

The sales manager said that when they went to the prospect's office, they asked the two questions and watched his body language for his responses.

"Are we still in the running to be your vendor?" was the first question.

The prospect leaned forward, spread his arms, palms open, smiled, nodded and said, "Of course."

Problem's Gift
Problem: a chance to do your best.
- Duke Ellington

Great signals. Leaning forward with spread arms is like reaching out to someone to hug them and welcome them into the family. Palms opened signaled he was being truthful. It's almost impossible for someone to lie to you with their palms exposed. The smile with teeth showing and nod were consistent with his other positive gestures.

The next question is what saved them $2000. I had told him to ask the prospect if he had the money in the budget and see what he did with his hands to his face.

"Can we assume you still have the money in the budget to go forward with the project?" the sales manager asked.

The prospect leaned back, dropped his chin, looked up and lightly touched the side of his nose, paused for a heartbeat, and replied, "No, it's not. We've made some changes."

The sales manager said that he and his salesman nearly fell out of their chairs laughing because they didn't think the prospect would do what I told them he would do.

Small children. Four or five years old. Have you ever seen what they do with their hands if you catch them in a big fib? Let's say I walk into my office, my grandson's back is to me, and he doesn't know I'm there. He knocks over my grandmother's vase and it shatters.

"Jake! Did you break that vase?"

He twirls around, surprised. "I didn't do it grandpa!" And he throws both hands up to cover his mouth. Like he's trying to shove the words back where they came from.

As we get older we become more sophisticated. Teenagers, if they're not telling the absolute truth, will touch their mouth around their lips.

When Jana was in junior high, I was talking to her the next day after her Friday night sleepover with her girlfriends.

"So-o-o, what did you guys do last night?" I asked.

Touching her upper lip, she replied, "We went to Beth's."

"No you didn't. What did you do last night?"

"We went to Tracy's?" she answered with less confidence, touching her lip again.

"Jana. One last chance. What did you guys do last night?"

Exasperated, she leaned forward, spread her arms, opened her palms, and said, "Geez, dad. We went to the movies. How did you know?"

Never tell a teenager how you know. Wait until they leave home.

But as we get older, we become even more sophisticated. Adults, if they have something to hide, will brush the tip of their nose or the side of their nose before they answer. That's what I told the guys in San Diego to look for.

Is the money in the budget? Just before the prospect denied it, he touched the side of his nose.

The sales manager remained calm. He said normally he would have tried to guess what the new budget was and drop the price by $2000 on his own initiative. But because he determined this was a negotiation tactic, he followed-up with a few well-placed questions.

Sure enough he discovered the prospect had moved the money from Budget A to Budget B. Just as easily, he could move the money back into Budget A.

The sales manager said, "That one touch of the nose saved us $2000."

People lie. Body language doesn't.

49

In Search of the Holy Grail

Treasure It. Guard It. But Use It.

A Dallas salesman spoke up from the back of the room at one of our seminars where we had several hundred people there that day.

"Jerry," he asked sincerely, "do you think there will ever be a day when salespeople can find customers without having to cold call?"

He asked the question I've been asking myself since I got into sales in 1973. Finding the answer to that question has been my search for the Holy Grail of sales.

"If I knew the answer, Dave," I assured him, "we wouldn't be sitting in this ballroom with a few hundred people in attendance. I could fill the entire Dallas Convention Center with thousands of people."

As long as you want customers, as long as you want to stay in sales, as long as you want to keep your business, you're going to have to cold call – like it or not. But as I mentioned at the beginning of the book, cold calling is only one of the many tools you have in your toolbox. Take advantage of every tool you have.

When you cold call, be direct. Ask for what you want. And what you want is to help other people improve their lives.

This book has given you hundreds of strategies, tactics, and techniques to improve your skills. In the Appendixes following this chapter you'll find more tools that will get you referrals, increase your customer retention, and position you to be #2 until you're #1.

This book has shown you what to do. How to do it. Why it works. The thirty years of experiences I've gained from my problems, failures, mistakes, and successes are now yours without you having to pay the heavy tolls in time and money they cost me. The knowledge that thousands of dedicated salespeople like you have shared with me belongs to you. Treasure it. Guard it. But use it.

Jon Kabat-Zin, author of *Wherever You Go There You Are*, said that "The best we can do is to show others what we have seen up to now. It's at best a progress report, a map of our experiences, by no means the absolute truth." I agree. Now you know what I've seen.

Have fun selling. I guarantee you're going to meet some interesting people along the way, have rich experiences to share with others, and learn more about yourself than you ever imagined. I know you'll be surprised and pleased to discover who you really are.

I'm Done
The point of good writing is knowing when to stop.
- L.M. Montgomery

A Program to Increase Your Referrals

Referral Secrets from the #1 Salesman in the World

Two of the biggest complaints business owners and sales managers have are that their salespeople are not (1) asking for the order, and (2) asking for referrals.

While at the Fortune 1000 McCaw Communications Telepage Northwest for four years, I led the nation for new business found through cold calling and referrals every year.

I learned the secrets of getting referrals from Joe Girard, *How to Sell Anything to Anybody*. His secrets continue to produce sales for me to this day. Girard's been listed in the *Guinness Book of World Records* for four consecutive years as the #1 Salesman in the World. He sold new cars, in of all places, Detroit, Michigan. Where anyone can get a good deal on a new car.

Why salespeople fail to get referrals

The salesperson's post-sale request, "If you know anyone who would be interested in buying what I sell, please tell them about me," is not a referral strategy.

Why doesn't the request work?

The customer is too preoccupied with her new purchase to think about giving referrals. Her excited mind is in one place, your referral request in another. She hasn't used your service or product yet. She doesn't know if you're going to fulfill your promises, and she doesn't want to jeopardize her friendships. In short, she's of no mind to give you any referrals – yet. But once the sale is made, the product delivered, the service performed – once the excitement of the new purchase has subsided – referrals flourish.

Until then, you must position yourself to get them.

The three secrets from the #1 Salesman in the World

1. Girard coined the phrase *The Law of 250*. The Law of 250 states that every person you know knows 250 others you don't. Girard found that working on this principle gives you leverage for creating new business and getting referrals. For example, if you have a customer base of 100 people, you have potential access to 25,000 others you don't know and will never meet.

2. Not everyone is buying what you're selling today. But at some point they – or some of their 250 friends – will. You need to communicate and stay connected to your customer base so they'll *remember* you first when they or their friends are ready to buy.

3. You must *keep in touch* in an engaging manner with every customer and prospect at least once a month. Any longer between contacts, you'll be forgotten. You must position and promote yourself so you'll be the first person they think about when your product or service is discussed.

   To keep in touch, Girard sent a card to his 13,000 customers and prospects every month with the simple message, "I like you. Joe Girard." His cards accomplished two things: (a) they sold Girard and the relationship – not the product; and (b) he got people to remember him first when they or their friends were ready to buy.

Before the cyber age, I modified Joe's idea of keeping in touch and designed my own Just a Thought...™ postcards. Being a photographer, I'd take my own pictures, provide a thoughtful quote beneath each photo, insert my business card information on the card, and deliver them to the printer.

The process, like Girard's, was time consuming and expensive: hours spent creating and addressing the cards, plus the printing and postage costs. But it was worth every hour and every stamp because my referrals and sales skyrocketed.

Then came the birth of the Internet and email. I converted my Just a Thought...™ postcards into our You've Got Contacts D-I-Y Sales & Marketing Email Postcards™ and have been able to make Girard's secrets available to thousands of salespeople, business owners, entrepreneurs, and professionals to increase their sales through referrals.

Your Name
Company Name
Street Address
City, State Zip Code
Phone Number
Fax Number
Email Address
Website Address

Illinois

Your personalized marketing message goes here.

At the historic state capitol in Springfield, Abraham Lincoln first delivered his famous "A house divided against itself cannot stand" speech.

Send weekly fun and entertaining email postcards to stay connected, increase referrals, cross-sell, increase customer retention, network, and position yourself to be #2 until you're #1.

How to get your own referral program

Visit our website at www.YouveGotContacts.com and sign-up for your free 30-day trial of hundreds of D-I-Y Sales & Marketing Email Postcards™ to send to every contact on a daily, weekly, or monthly basis to increase your sales. The email postcards supplement your cold calling and networking activities and allow you to stay connected with every person until they're ready to buy or give you referrals.

For detailed information on how this sales and marketing tool works, download my free ebook *Selling without Cold Calling? – the Holy Grail of Selling*, at our website and read the chapter "Referrals Grow on Trees".

Appendix B

Positioning Yourself to Be #2

How to Make the Short List
Without Becoming a Pest

How many times have you had the courage to cold call, find a prospect, make a presentation, and give a proposal only to be told at the last minute, "Sorry. We've decided to wait until next year. Why don't you call me back in six months?"

You bite your lip and fight back the tears.

"Okay," you whimper.

But you're smart. You call back in five.

"Oh, man, I wished you'd have called last week. We just bought your product from your competitor."

"Why didn't you call me?" you ask, trying to hide your disappointment.

"Sorry. We simply forgot about you. We lost your proposal. And we haven't heard from you for months. Didn't know how to find you."

You've witnessed the birth of the concept of my You've Got Contacts D-I-Y Sales & Marketing Email Postcards™. I got so tired of losing business like this because people forgot about me, that I had to come up with a plan to make sure they'd never forget again.

This rejection was the meeting of three simultaneous events – the perfect sales storm. I'd been brainstorming for how to increase my referrals when I came across Joe Girard's *How to Sell Anything to Anybody* (see Appendix A). And I was familiar with Harvey Mackay's admonishment to position myself to be #2; but I didn't know how.

255

Then came the catalyst of losing the prospect because he forgot about me. Driving away from my lost account, the picture of the Just a Thought...™ postcards (Appendix A) came to me. The post-cards led to the creation of another business, You've Got Contacts, which gave us the opportunity to help thousands of people in business position themselves to get ahead of the competition.

If you're tired of losing prospects, and if you want to position yourself to be #2 when change is made, go to www.YouveGot Contacts.com and sign up for your free 30-day trial of the D-I-Y Sales & Marketing Email Postcards™ to see for yourself how easy it is to create top-of-mind awareness while eliminating the competition. See **Appendix A** for an example of hundreds of cards to select from.

For detailed information about the program, download my free ebook, *Selling without Cold Calling? – the Holy Grail of Selling*, at our website and read the chapter "Birth Is a Scream".

Increasing Customer Retention

It's About Staying Connected

The *Harvard Business Review* published a Bain & Co. study that found: (a) it is 6-7 times more expensive to gain a new customer than it is to retain an existing customer; (b) U.S. companies lose 50% of their customers every 5 years; and (c) a 5% increase in customer retention can increase profits by 25% - 95%.

Sales & Marketing Magazine found that the #1 reason customers leave is because the salesperson lost contact with them. Not because they got a lower price, a better product, or better service. But because the salesperson simply lost contact. An easy, low-cost, fixable problem.

Jeffrey Gitomer, *The Little Black Book of Connections: 6.5 Assets for Networking Your Way to Rich Relationships*, said that, "Staying in touch is more important and more valuable than making the initial connection." He said to send a "weekly tip or tidbit of useful information…to every customer, every week."

Three lines of defense

There are three lines of defense for keeping the customers you have.

Salespeople have the primary responsibility for keeping their accounts. They found them and sold them, so they should be the first charged with keeping them.

Because management's income is tied directly to keeping accounts, they're the second line of defense. They also need to control situations where their salespeople might get recruited by the competition and leave. Too little, too late, they realize that the relationship the customer had with the company followed the salesperson out the door like a shadow. Rarely is management on a first name basis with their customers. They've probably never met them. Even if they can find their files, a file is not a relationship. Competitors will be called, profits will evaporate. Yet this is a low-maintenance problem with an inexpensive remedy.

The last line of defense for keeping customers belongs to the service department. They need to develop relationships in order to both cross-sell new services and to increase customer retention. Many of a company's sales and profits are made and lost in service. Service people are salespeople without portfolio. Yes, they'll gripe because they don't get the commissions of the salespeople. But they have as much responsibility for keeping their jobs as does management and sales. Besides, they could turn the double-play and introduce the salespeople to customers they've never met who come through the service department's back door.

A better way to sell without having to cold call

How do sales, management, and service increase customer retention? Have each department send one D-I-Y Sales & Marketing Email Postcard™ (available at www.YouveGotContacts.com) each month to every person in their database to cross-sell, renew service contracts, and thank customers for their continued business. See **Appendix A** for an example of hundreds of cards to select from.

Not only will the email postcards cut new customer acquisition costs, increase customer retention, and increase profits, but salespeople will be excited because they've found another way to increase their sales without having to continually cold call.

For detailed information for how to increase your customer retention rate, and to learn more about how the D-I-Y Sales & Marketing Email Postcards™ can help, download my free ebook, *Selling without Cold Calling? – the Holy Grail of Selling*, at our website and read the chapter "Let's Talk About Retention – Customer Not Water".

Do Not Call Registry

Didn't the Federal Government Ban Cold Calling?

You wish.

The Federal government's position on cold calling is that it applies ONLY if you call people on their *personal home phone* numbers and on their *personal cell phone* numbers. It has no effect on business-to-business cold calls. See www.ftc.gov for complete legal and up-to-date information.

Who's hurt the most by the DNCR? Mostly residential real estate salespeople and investment and financial consultants. Charities are exempt from the DNCR as well as politicians who wrote the law (wouldn't you know).

Of course, salespeople affected by the DNCR have even more incentive to network and get referrals. For networking and referral programs that produce results, see **Appendixes A-C**.

At www.YouveGotContacts.com you can download my free ebook *Selling without Cold Calling? – the Holy Grail of Selling* to get networking and referral programs.

Index

A

ACT!, 52
Alessandra, Tony, 197
Amazing Face Reading, 183
Amazing Kreskin, 239
Arafat, Yassar, 210

B

Bandler, Richard, 14
batter's box, 9, 15
be #2 until you're #1, 144, 148, 250
   do business with your competitor,
     146
   not interested, 148
   pilot project, 144, 145
   slow approach, 146, 147, 148
Beckwith, Harry, 171
believe, 7, 124-128
   what to believe, 126
Blanchard, Kenneth, 160
body language, 18, 19, 71, 73, 130,
   134, 175, 241-244, 246, 248
   Harding, Tonya, 241
   pain in the neck, 242
   raised steeple, 244
   scratches neck, 243
   touch of the nose, 248
Burg, Bob, 178, 181

C

#1 complaint of customers, 37
   6 Second technique, 38
   interruptions, 37, 38, 39
   Pease, Barbara and Allan, 37
   Shafir, Rebecca Z., 37
call reluctance, 7, 14, 20
   courage to act, 7, 16
Carson, Johnny, 239
Cialdini, Robert, and *Influence*, 35, 40,
   165
cold calling definition, 3
   aliases, 4
   cross-selling, 6
   networking, 5, 173, 207, 219, 254,
    260

   referrals, 6, 10, 91, 164, 250-255,
    260
   trade show, 5, 8, 173, 176-177, 234
Cold Calling for Cowards®, 8, 22, 109,
   131, 213
commitment and consistency, 40, 41-
   45, 47, 55, 80, 89, 90, 133, 141,
   147, 148, 156, 157, 162, 167, 245
   Chinese brainwashing technique, 40
   Cialdini, Robert, 40
   homework, 44, 122, 133
   qualifying questions, 42, 44, 45, 47,
    192
count the F's, 116
coward, 20-22, 24
   semper fi, 20, 24
   U.S. Marines, 24
customer retention, 52, 96, 250, 257-
   259
   Gitomer, Jeffrey, 257
   keeping the customers, 257
   management, 257, 258
   salespeople, 257, 258
   service, 258

D

dealing with rejection, 16
   Closer technique, 17
   Find the Quarter techique, 17
   Fonz technique, 18
   President Jeb Bartlett technique, 16
decision-maker, 5, 51, 56, 77, 80-83,
   87, 88, 97- 99,101, 113, 145, 154,
   155, 159, 168, 203, 204, 213, 221
Definitive Book of Body Language, 213
Dimitrius, Jo-Ellan, 198
D-I-Y Sales & Marketing Email
   Postcards™, 88, 253-256, 258-259
Do Not Call Registry, 260
Drawing on the Right Side of the Brain,
   117

E

Edwards, Betty, 117
Endless Referrals, 178

F

5% salesperson, 81
fear of rejection, 3, 7, 13, 14. 16, 19
finding customers, 11
Fulfer, Mac, 183

G

gatekeeper, 57, 79, 82-85, 87, 91, 95-96, 134, 155, 157, 175, 234
gatekeeper techniques, 82
    Big Apple technique, 86
    Brotherly Love technique, 86
    Chamber of Commerce technique, 88
    Contact Us technique, 89
    GM technique, 90-92
    Paul Revere technique, 84
    Second City technique, 85
    Space Needle technique, 86
Get Anyone to Do Anything, 166
get calls taken and returned, 159
    Because technique, 165
    Cheese technique, 160
    Fork technique, 159
    Just So You Know technique, 166
    Law of Reciprocation technique, 163
    Negotiating for Discount technique, 163
    Simple technique, 162
    Skeletons in the Closet technique, 167
    Who Moved My Cheese?, 160
Girard, Joe, 251-253
Gitomer, Jeffrey, 257
give up calling?, 114
    magic number, 114
Gladwell, Malcolm, 59
    Blink, 59
Glass, Dr. Lillian, 34
Griffey, Ken Jr., 26, 27
Grinder, John, 14
Grissom, Gil, 95, 199

H

handshakes, 207, 210-213, 216, 221, 224, 236, 240
    60 Minutes, 210
    Arafat, Yassar, 210
    Bone-Crusher, 232-233
    Clinton, Bill, 210-211
    Dead Fish, 220-222, 237, 240
    Dominant, 214, 217, 219
    double handshake, 223-225
    Farmer in the Dell, 231
    Florida Highway Patrol, 232
    Half-Hand, 228-231, 237
    Karzai, Hamid, 211
    men initiate, 236
    Musharraf, General Pervez, 211
    Palm Down, 213-215, 217-219, 240
    Palm Up, 216, 218, 219
    Patton, George, 214
    physical limitations, 222
    physically challenged, 237
    Politician, 223, 230
    Rabin, Yitzhak, 210
    shake or not, 234
    submissive, 214, 217-219
    Traveling Arm, 226
    two counter tactics, 214
Harding, Tonya, 241
Holy Grail of Sales, 249

I

increasing customer retention, 52, 257
    Bain & Co. study, 52, 257
    Harvard Business Review, 52, 257

J

Johnson, Randy, 9, 25
Johnson, Spencer, 160

L

Langer, Ellen, 165-166
Leno, Jay, 227
letter, 103, 106-108, 109
    Spence, Padraic, 106
    Williams, Roy H., 107
Letterman, David, 227
Level 1 prospect. *See* three levels of prospects
Level 2 prospect. *See* three levels of prospects
Level 3 prospect. *See* three levels of prospects

Lieberman, Dr. David J., 166
Little Black Book of Connections, 257
Lorayne, Harry, 35, 179, 181
Los Angeles Times, 268

M

Martinez, Edgar, 25-28
   make contact with the ball, 27
McCaw Communications, 11, 53, 122,
   152, 174, 251, 268
McCaw, Craig, 50
mirror, 60, 61
mirror image, 187, 201,202
   two part technique, 188
Motorola, 88, 127

N

Nemko, Dr. Marty, 22
Neuro-Linguistic Programming, 14

O

objections, 137, 141-143, 244
   oh?, 137-138

P

paradox of cold calling, 31-32
   eliminate prospects, 32
   strategic goals, 31
   tactical goals, 31
paradoxical intention, 20-24
   Frankl, Dr. Viktor, 20-22
   logotherapy, 20, 21
Patton, General George, 214
Pease, Allan, 214, 226, 239
Pease, Barbara and Allan, 37, 90, 213
   Why Men Don't Listen and Women
     Can't Read Maps, 37, 90
Peoples, David, 198
personalities, 63, 97, 111, 113, 194,
   197, 199, 201, 203-204, 206, 215
   Amiable, 113-115, 198-200, 202,
     204
   Analytical, 112-115, 139, 168, 198,
     199, 201-203, 206
   best question to ask, 111, 115
   chameleons, 200

Driver, 112-115, 195, 196, 198,
   199, 200-204, 215
Expressive, 113, 115, 198, 199, 200,
   203-206
Magic 6 questions, 193
Platinum Rule, 197
Polyani, Michael, 130
positioning yourself to be #2, 51, 255
   Mackay, Harvey, 51, 144, 255
prepare for appointment, 130, 132
   seven steps, 132-133
   graphic, 133
   Intuitive technique, 130, 132, 135,
     136
Princeton University, 59
   Psychological Science, 59
   Todorov, Alex, 59
psychics, psychos, and Columbo, 149
   Columbo technique, 154
   cut you off at the knees, 149, 157

R

Reading People, 198
remember names, 178, 179
   five things you need to do, 181-184
Remembering People, 179
ride-alongs, 129, 130
Ruth, Babe, 15
Rx for listening, 33
   Glass, Dr. Lillian, 34
   Golden Pad technique, 35
   student lectures, 35

S

#1 Salesman in the World, 10, 251-252
   Girard, Joe, 251-253
   Guinness Book of World Records,
     251
   Law of 250, 252
script, 64, 75-81, 174
   extemporaneous, 76, 79
   spontaneous, 76
   vocal suicide, 64, 65
Seinfeld, Jerry, 118
Selling Power, 96
Selling the Invisible, 171
Selling to the Top, 198
Selling without Cold Calling? - the
   Holy Grail of Selling, 254

Shafir, Rebecca Z., 37
smiling, 60
Solicitors Will Be Shot, 1
stalker, 56, 168-170
Stevens, Mark, 6
Stewart, Jon, 227
stupid things, 119, 171
    during an interview, 119-120

T

30-second commercial, 172
    face-to-face, 173
    telephone, 172
    trade show, 176
    walk-in cold call, 174
telephone headset, 72
    Bluetooth, 73
    Dork Factor, 72, 73
    GN Netcom, 73
    Plantronics, 73
three levels of prospects, 48
    Level 1 prospect, 48-49
    Level 2 prospect, 8, 49, 51-52, 114,
       146, 175, 176
    Level 3 prospect, 49, 175
three reasons cold calling doesn't work,
    10
three things customers buy, 59
    benefits or opportunities, 60
    buying into the problem, 62
    buys you, 59
    decision based upon trust, 60
three things to do when cold calling, 52
    ACT!, 52
    identify, 52
    keep in touch, 55, 114, 118, 146,
       168, 169, 252
    keep records, 52, 146
time to cold call, 28, 172
    3800/6 technique, 29
    5-Minute technique, 29
Tomatis, Dr. Alfred, 73
turn cold calls into appointments, 118
    beliefs, 122, 126, 127
    foot out of your mouth, 118, 120
    good first impression, 118, 120
    lack of confidence, 122
    not doing our homework, 122

    not studying the psychology of
      selling, 122
    think on your feet, 118, 138

V

voice, 60, 64, 65, 67, 70-73, 77, 86
    Barr, Rosanne, 70
    Clooney, George, 70
    Darth Vader, 69
    Godfried, Gilbert, 70
    hands behind your back, 71
    inflections, 68, 73
    Jones, James Earl, 69
    MONSTER TRUCK
      EXTRAVAGANZA, 67
    Mullally, Megan, 69
    pause, 68
    rate of delivery, 68
    Roberts, Julia, 70, 184
    stand up, 70, 71, 73
    weight on one foot, 70
voicemail, 84, 87, 90-91, 93-98, 100-
    104, 113, 118, 149, 156
    blog, 91, 97, 176
    chambers of commerce, 104
    frequency of contact, 78, 96
    Gallup Organization, 99
    leave it?, 93
    looking for clues, 95
    sell one of three things, 94
    trick a prospect, 99
    voicemail script, 103
    what decision-makers look for, 98
    Wizard of Ads, 103
    www.historychannel.com, 97

W

Westin Hotels, 181
Williams, Roy H., 103, 107, 109

Y

Your Marketing Sucks, 6
YouveGotContacts.com, 177, 254

Z

Zen Master of Cold Calls, 268

BIBLIOGRAPHY

Alessandra, T. and O'Conner, M. *The Platinum Rule: Discover the Four Basic Business Personalities and How They Can Lead You to Success*, Walden Books, Inc., 1996.

Bandler, R. and Grinder, J. *The Structure of Magic: A Book About Language and Therapy*, Science and Behavior Books, 1976.

Beckwith, H. *What Clients Love – A Field Guide to Growing Your Business*, Warner Business Books, 2003.

Burg, B. *Endless Referrals*, McGraw-Hill, 1999.

Buzan, T. *The Mind Map Book: How to Use Radiant Thinking to Maximize Your Brain's Untapped Potential*, Plume, 1996.

Cialdini, R. *Influence: Science and Practice*, Allyn and Bacon, 2001.

Cialdini, R. *Influence: The Power of Persuasion*, William Morrow and Company, Inc., 1993.

Daley, K. *Socratic Selling: How to Ask Questions That Get the Sale*, McGraw-Hill, 1996.

Dawson, R. *Secrets of Power Persuasion – Everything You'll Ever Need to Get Anything You'll Ever Want*, Prentice Press, 1992.

Dimitrius, J. and Mazzarella, M. *Reading People: How to Understand People and Predict Their Behavior – Anytime, Anyplace.* The Ballentine Publishing Group, 1999.

Edwards, B. *Drawing on the Right Side of the Brain*, Tarcher, 1999.

Frankl, V. *Man's Search for Meaning*, Pocket Press, 1985.

Fulfer, M. *Amazing Face Reading: An Illustrated Encyclopedia for Reading Faces*, Creative Alternatives, 1996.

Girard, J. and Brown, S. *How to Sell Anything to Anybody*, Warner Books, 1977.

Gitomer, J. *The Little Black Book of Connections: 6.5 Assets for Networking Your Way to Rich Relationships*, Bard Press, 2006.

Gladwell, M. *Blink: The Power of Thinking Without Thinking*, Little Brown and Company, 2005.

Glass, L. *Talk to Win – Six Steps to a Successful Vocal Image*, Putnam Publishing Group, 1988.

Godin, S. *Permission Marketing*, Simon & Schuster, 1999.

Johnson, S. *Who Moved My Cheese? – An Amazing Way to Deal with Change in Your Work and in Your Life*, Putnam, 1998.

Kenley, J. *Voice Power: Using Your Voice to Captivate, Persuade, and Command Attention*, American Management Association, 2002.

Khalsa, M. *Let's Get Real or Let's Not Play*, Franklin Covey, 1999.

Lieberman, D. *Get Anyone to Do Anything*, St. Martin's Press, 2000.

Mackay, H. *Swim with the Sharks without Being Eaten Alive: Outsell, Outmanage, Outmotivate, and Outnegotiate Your Competition*, Ballentine Books, 1988.

Michaelson, G. and Michaelson, S. *Sun Tzu Strategies for Selling, How to Use the Art of War to Build Lifelong Customer Relationships*, McGraw-Hill, 2004.

Nelson, W. and Pipkin, T. *The Tao of Willie: A Guide to the Happiness in Your Heart*, Gotham Books, 2006.

Pease, A. and Pease, B. *The Definitive Book of Body Language*, Bantam Dell, 2006.

Pease, A. and Pease, B. *Why Men Don't Listen and Women Can't Read Maps: How We're Different and What to Do About It*, Welcome Rain Publishers, 2000.

Penick, H. and Shrake, B. *And If You Play Golf, You're My Friend*, Simon & Schuster, 1992.

Penick, H. and Shrake, B. *The Wisdom of Harvey Penick*, Simon & Schuster, 1997.

Peoples, D. *Selling to the Top: David Peoples' Executive Selling Skills*, Wiley, 1993.

RoAne, S. *How to Create Your Own Luck: the "You Never Know" Approach to Networking, Taking Chances, and Opening Yourself to Opportunity*, John Wiley & Sons, 2004.

RoAne, S. *How to Work a Room: The Ultimate Guide to Savvy Socializing in Person and Online*, Collins, 2000.

Rotella, B. and Cullen, B. *Golf Is Not a Game of Perfect*, Simon & Schuster, 1995.

Shafir, R. *The Zen of Listening: Mindful Communication in the Age of Distraction*, The Theosophical Publishing House, 2000.

Spence, P. *Write Smart and Get Decisions: The Complete Guide to Business Writing*, The Water Street Press, 1996.

Stevens, M. *Your Marketing Sucks*, Three Rivers Press, 2005.

Tracy, B. *Goals: How to Get Everything You Want – and Faster Than You Thought Possible*, Berrett-Koehler Publishers, 2003.

Yaverbaum, E. and Shook, R. *I'll Get Back to You: 156 Ways to Get People to Return Your Calls and Other Helpful Tips*, McGraw-Hill, 1996.

Williams, R. *The Wizard of Ads: Turning Words into Magic and Dreamers into Millionaires*, Bard Press, 1998.

Ziglar, Z. *See You at the Top: 25th Anniversary Edition*, Pelican Publishing Company, 2000.

Okay. Who's Responsible for This?

I've been compared to David Letterman.

Salesman since 1973. Business owner since 1992. Salesman-founder-president Jerry Hocutt of Hocutt & Associates, Inc. Why I go to work every day: to help people in business find, sell to, and retain customers.

I've trained over 150,000 salespeople, business owners, entrepreneurs, professionals, and managers in our nationally acclaimed Cold Calling for Cowards® seminars. ("He's the Zen Master of Cold Calls" – *Los Angeles Times*.)

I've been compared to David Letterman by the *New Brunswick (NJ) Star-Ledger* ("Lord of the Rings"). "Okay, so he's not David Letterman." I didn't say it was flattering. Just that I've been compared to him.

The #1 Salesman in the Nation and Salesman of the Year for three years at the then Fortune 1000 McCaw Communications' Telepage Northwest.

I've had successful sales careers in school pictures, office equipment, 2-way radios, pagers and cellular phones, sales seminars, and Internet marketing. Go figure.

Husband of one, father of 2, father-in-law to 2, grandfather of 4, and harassed by one granddog.

Subscribe to my free sales and marketing newsletter – *Snippets*. Go to www.ColdCallingForCowards.com and sign-up today.

Interview the Author

Invite Me to Your Sales Meeting

For your next sales meeting, put me on your speakerphone and let your salespeople ask me questions about my book. Visit our website and see how you and your staff can interview me for your next meeting.

> "Books by experts do have an influence, especially to people over 30. Books have built-in credibility – unfortunately, they're more credible than you are. You could say something a hundred times and no one pays attention, but if the same advice is in a book, suddenly it's taken seriously."
>
> —*Your Attention, Please.*
> Paul B. Brown and Alison Davis

Media Requests?

If you'd like to interview me for your broadcasts, magazine, or newspaper, visit our website or email me for more information.

Need Content for Your Newspaper or Newsletter?

Visit our website and download my free articles.

www.ColdCallingForCowards.com
jerry.cec@coldcallingforcowards.com

Need a Speaker for Your Next Event?

Whether you need a keynote, seminar, or breakout speaker for your next event, visit www.ColdCallingForCowards.com for more information or call 800-378-5941.

Some of Jerry's thousands of Cold Calling for Cowards® seminar attendees:

Bank of America · Coldwell Banker · UPS · FedEx · Pepsi Cola Verizon Wireless · Nextel · Sprint · IBM · Xerox · Coca Cola · ADP · Merrill Lynch · Paine Webber · SBC Communications · Morgan Stanley · Office Depot · Washington Mutual · Dell · State Farm · Marriott · GE · Hyatt · Ritz-Carlton · Farmers Insurance · U.S. Marines · U.S. Navy · U.S. Army · Clear Channel · Blue Man Group · Chicago Title · MTM Recognition · University of Maryland Los Angeles Times · Seattle Times · Dallas Morning News · The Press Enterprise · St. Petersburg Times · Key Bank · Wells Fargo Bank · U.S. Bank · Gallup Organization · San Jose State University Westin Hotels · Hilton Hotels · PEMCO Insurance · New York Life · Allstate · AFLAC · Avaya · First Third Bank · Pre-Paid Legal · Xpedx · Shred-It · Addecco Staffing · LaSalle Bank · Provident Bank · Boeing · Aramark · Motorola · Pfizer · CB Richard Ellis · Johnson & Johnson · Edward Jones · Kinko's · Minolta · Time Warner · U.S. Post Office · Manpower · Staples · Safeco · Wachovia

Everybody Has a Story

Let's hear it. Send me your best sales or cold calling stories. It could be in my next book and you'll get more than your 15 minutes of fame. You'll be forever.

What funny thing happened to you on a sales call? Or a cold call? What horror stories have you experienced and survived (or not)?

What did you learn from a prospect, customer, or salesperson that's made your life easier? What suggestions would you give someone new starting out?

What's been your most difficult lesson? What clues do you look for on a sales call? What surprised you the most? How do you deal with the fear of rejection? How do you deal with objections?

How do you get people to take your calls? Return your calls? How do you deal with voicemail and email? How do you get referrals? Get people to remember you when they finally decide to buy?

What questions would you like to have answered? What books inspire you? What sales training would you recommend to others?

I really want to know. Send me an email at my address below and put on the subject line: Have I Got a Story for You!

I look forward to hearing about and sharing your experiences.

Jerry
jerry.cec@coldcallingforcowards.com

Get Your Foot in the Door

Have some key accounts you'd like to crack? Can't get your prospects to consider changing vendors? People won't take or return your calls?

Maybe you work trade shows and want to get visitors to stop by your booth long enough to speak with you. Or you want them to take your call when you follow-up the lead.

> Send your prospects a personally autographed copy of
> *Cold Calling for Cowards*
> by Jerry Hocutt

Chances are your prospects have salespeople, too. Like you, they're looking for ideas that will help them improve their sales and motivate their staffs.

Tell your prospects you'll exchange a copy of *Cold Calling for Cowards* for fifteen minutes of their time. It's that easy to get your foot in the door.

Place a few Post-It® notes to chapters you know they'll like and tell them you'll call next week to get their thoughts. Every time they look at the book, they'll remember you.

Autographed copies come in bulk purchases with quantity discounts only when you order them through our website at www.ColdCallingForCowards.com. Give the books as gifts or use them for fund-raising or educational training purposes.

For additional copies of

Cold Calling for Cowards

How to Turn the Fear of Rejection into Opportunities, Sales, and Money

($21.95 paperback)

visit your favorite bookstore

order from Amazon.com or BarnesandNoble.com

visit ColdCallingForCowards.com

or call 800-378-5941

Visa / MasterCard / American Express accepted

Quantity discounts available

Chugwater Publishing
Phone: 253-639-0744
Fax: 253-630-4948
marketing@ChugwaterPublishing.com

Also bulk and individual orders
and autographed copies at our website
www.ColdCallingForCowards.com